Trout Fishing Guide

John Kent

HR

Acknowledgements

Information for this book has been obtained from a number of anglers and farmers. For their invaluable knowledge and friendship I would like specifically to thank a long-time angling companion, Dr Barney Mowat, of Whataroa; Steve Barclay, retired superintendent of Grey Hospital, now of Cambridge; Bill Barclay, of the Department of Conservation, Neils Beach; and Mike Thomas, of Killermont Station, Omarama.

Jody Richardson, fisheries research officer for the Ministry of Agriculture and Fisheries, kindly supplied drift dive figures for a number of rivers. My wife, Deirdre, and daughter Susanna, Don Rocard and Alison Roberton, of Auckland, helped with the photography.

Finally, I am greatly indebted to my angling and travelling companions and to the farmers of the South Island who without exception generously gave permission to cross their land and explore the wonderful rivers and lakes of the South Island.

Published by Heinemann Reed, a division of Octopus Publishing Group (NZ) Ltd, 39 Rawene Road, Birkenhead, Auckland. Associated companies, branches and representatives throughout the world.

ISBN 0 7900 0131 4

First published 1990

Typeset by Glenfield Graphics
Printed in Singapore

Contents

Foreword

When I reviewed John Kent's previous book, the companion volume *North Island Trout Fishing Guide*, for the *Listener*, I wrote: 'His curiosity about what lies around the next bend and his pleasure at visiting new water with old friends is as strong as ever. With any luck that curiosity and pleasure will take him around a few more bends in the South Island and we'll have the definitive trout fishing guide to the whole country.'

Well, his curiosity *did* take him round a few more bends in the South Island — 6 500 kilometres of them, to be precise. Those thousands of kilometres were covered by John in a six-week period in January and February of 1990, in the company, at various times, of two nephews, his son, his wife and daughter and a couple of good friends — and his 82-year-old mother, who was game enough to be flown in to the Haast in a doorless chopper! Having once attempted to keep up with John's 10-league boots, I'm not at all surprised at the distance he covered in that short period, nor at the rapid turnover of his companions!

But that fleeting visit merely complemented John's already comprehensive background knowledge of the wilds of the South Island. Born and brought up in Christchurch, he went to medical school in Dunedin, completed his house surgeon 'apprenticeship' in Nelson, and was later resident doctor on the hospital ship the *Wanganella* at Deep Cove in Manapouri. From each of these bases he tramped and fished extensively, building up an expertise as a fly fisherman and a knowledge of the country that shines through on every page of this guide.

About the only thing this book doesn't do is give the reader the rare privilege of watching the author working a pool: entering from the downstream run, wielding his carbon-fibre rod like a wand,

Opposite: La Fontaine, a famous fly fishing stream at Harihari.

whipping huge spools of line back and forth in the sky, missing overhanging bush by carefully judged centimetres until he's played the line out to the length he wants, then casting it forward in an arc so the trace lies down on the water like a feather on steel, finishing at the trout's tail with the last metres of invisible nylon flicking ahead, dropping the fly enticingly in front of the unsuspecting fish's mouth.

Despite John's mastery of casting technique, the book gives the lie to the idea of fishing as a mechanical process of throwing a piece of nylon into a river. John paints a picture of all the variables of the ecosystem which affect the fish, from climate to terrain, from water catchment changes to insect hatch, and it becomes clear that, for John at least, fishing is part of a wider communion with nature.

John's concern for the environment comes through strongly on every page of the book. His perspective on the land he describes here is very different from that of many other users, and is doubly valuable because of that — for he may see dangers in changing water quality before other land users.

I think John does our wildest places a service with this book. He looks at and describes these places with a loving and careful eye, detailing not only their fishing properties but also practical advice on access, permission, safety and gear. In doing that he underscores the value of the resource and seeks to safeguard its bounty for the future.

Greg McGee
April 1990

Introduction

This book is designed to help those anglers who enjoy exploring and fishing new water. I hope it will also encourage those who enjoy fishing the same streams to branch out and widen their horizons. Many anglers fish the same stream year after year, even fishing the same stretch of water on that stream and expecting that stream to remain constant. If winter floods have changed their favourite pool, they are filled with disappointment. But surely one of the excitements of trout fishing is the experience of a new stream or lake. Strange waters increase your feelings of expectancy.

Every new stretch of water presents new challenges, and one cannot criticise an angler for doing badly on unfamiliar waters. But what if an angler does badly on familiar water? I have yet to meet an unsuccessful angler who didn't have a good excuse: You should have been here on Thursday! The water is too clear; the stream is too low; the day's too bright; the wind's too strong; or the fish are simply not feeding. A bad angler will rarely succeed no matter how often he or she explores a stretch of water. A good angler is a good angler anywhere, even on strange waters. However, one can only learn and improve through new experiences. So take a risk! Try a new river. You may be pleasantly surprised. You may even have more success than on waters you fish regularly. Then again, if the scenery is beautiful and you are at peace with the world, what does it really matter?

Have you noticed that when you're concentrating on fishing all other troublesome thoughts rapidly evaporate? Why does the day pass so quickly? To the observant nature lover, no sport affords so much pleasure. At times the excitement can be intense. Imagine, after scrambling for an hour up a back-country river, you finally spot a magnificent wild trout swinging from side to side in the current, feeding. There's plenty of time, no other angler within miles. A careful plan of attack is called for.

First find a place downstream, sheltered from view by riverbank scrub, and watch the trout's feeding pattern, observing the direction of the breeze and the flow of the current. Is the fish nymphing or rising and feeding on surface flies? What are the insects being consumed? Do you have an artificial in your fly box resembling these tiny morsels? 'Will I scare the fish with a weighted nymph or is there sufficient ripple on the water to accommodate an inaccurate cast? Should I lengthen the trace so as not to line the fish, and also allow time for the nymph to sink to the same level as the trout?' You select a fly and notice that your hand shakes a little as you tie it carefully on to the delicate leader. Now is the moment to put your plan into action.

Keeping low, you creep up behind this magnificent wild fish, strip line off the reel and prepare to cast. Suddenly, you feel a surge of adrenalin. Your heart beats loud enough for the fish to hear, your mouth dries up and all sorts of doubts cross your mind. 'Have I selected the right fly? Why will the fish take my artificial in preference to natural insects? Is 2.5 kg strength nylon sufficiently strong to hold this fish? What if it turns when hooked and races downstream through the rapids? Can I cast with sufficient accuracy to avoid that overhanging beech tree? Should I even attempt to cast after clumsily putting down that last fish? I'm sure to botch it!'

Just at that crucial moment, a cloud darkens the sky and the fish is lost momentarily from view. You wait patiently in cold, knee-deep water and ponder the words you have heard for years from non-angling friends. 'Fishing must be dull and boring.' 'I haven't the patience.' 'You've been away all day and returned with nothing. What have you been doing?' And here you are, standing knee deep in this cold mountain river, shivering with nervous tension! Who said trout fishing is relaxing?

Suddenly, the light returns and, thankfully, your fish is still there. You begin false casting, carefully measuring the distance between you and the fish. With great care, knowing that one mistake will frighten the fish into the depths of the pool, you gently land the deception in the right place. The artificial drifts down naturally with the current and without a moment's hesitation the fish swings across and sucks in your fly. You lift the rod and tighten, feeling the weight of the fish. That is the essence of fly fishing – the moment of take. All hell breaks loose as the fish dashes madly upstream, stripping line off the screaming reel.

Wild trout in a wild river seldom give up easily. The play is only over when, after a good tussle, the fish is gently beached and then released, unharmed, to swim slowly back into the depths of the pool. Now for that hot thermos of coffee, ideally shared with a friend. And as your pulse gradually settles back to normal you reflect on what a wonderful day it is!

I make no excuse for emphasising fly fishing in this book. Once an angler has developed fly-casting skills, and they are not difficult to learn, there is just no comparison with spin or bait fishing. The pure excitement of watching a trout move sideways to take your nymph, feeling the tug when a fish grabs your wet fly or lure on the swing, or watching it rise to sip in your dry fly cannot be matched by any other fishing method. However, despite these comments, there is a definite place for spinning and live-bait fishing, especially for junior anglers. I certainly caught fish by both these methods before mastering a fly rod.

At times, a river may be totally unsuitable for fly fishing, yet trout can still be caught on a spinner. As a teenager I had thought of fly fishing as too difficult to learn! It isn't, especially if you can find another fly fisher with the time and patience to start you off. It is much easier to learn from an experienced angler than from a book.

One of the charms of trout fishing is that if you live to be a hundred you'll never learn it all. There are so many constantly changing parameters affecting trout environment, trout food and the trout themselves. Such variables as season, barometric pressure, temperature, wind direction and velocity, light intensity, time of day, the colour and state of the water and insect hatch are but a few of the factors affecting the catch rate. You may catch a limit one day but return empty handed the next, even though fishing the same spot.

The geography and climate of the South Island are extraordinarily varied, the snow-covered alps, dark, dripping rainforests, fertile plains, dry, barren deserts and rugged coastlines all within a few kilometres of each other. Annual rainfall can be as high as 6 000 mm in Fiordland and as low as 250 mm some 60 kilometres to the east in Central Otago. The prevailing winds are the nor'westers sweeping across the Tasman Sea and collecting water to dump on the West Coast. On the eastern side of the Southern Alps the nor'wester is a strong, warm, dry wind. These winds usually herald the arrival of a cold front, and the development of a sou'wester after the front passes can drop the temperature by as much as 12 degrees C in a couple of hours.

The wide variations in land forms and climate are naturally reflected by the waterways. There are sluggish rain- and swamp-fed streams meandering across farmland, clear rushing mountain torrents shaded by dense native bush, unstable glacier-fed rivers, cold spring streams and natural as well as man-made lakes. Nearly all the South Island's waterways contain trout, and in some remote areas fish weighing 4.5 kg are not uncommon.

Many of the relatively inaccessible headwaters in the Southern Alps may see no anglers from one year to the next. Yet with so many rivers and lakes exhibiting such widely differing characteristics, the South Island is truly an angler's paradise. Over 270 rivers and 95 lakes are described in this book and it would take a lifetime to fish even half of the water. Although most of the worthwhile rivers and lakes in the South Island are mentioned, some excellent small local streams may well have been missed. On the other hand some anglers may be disappointed to find their special spot described. I apologise for this, but hopefully anglers fishing 'your' stream will practise catch-and-release conservation methods. (May I suggest you pay a reciprocal visit to *their* stream!) Many of these rivers contain only small stocks of trout and can easily be fished out. Only the larger lakes can withstand the removal of larger numbers of fish, and even here it is wasteful and selfish to take more than a few. These last comments are especially directed towards those anglers using helicopters to visit inaccessible waters.

Trout populations in some of the rivers described have been assessed by biologists employed by the Ministry of Agriculture and Fisheries using drift diving techniques. These figures are included when available, but they should be taken as a guide only. It is obviously impossible to survey a whole river, and fish will move upstream or downstream according to the season and weather conditions. However, it is reassuring to know that the new water you are exploring for the first time probably contains a good population of trout.

Before venturing onto a new stream, it is well worth buying an up-to-date map of the area. These are produced by the Department of Survey and Land Information and are available at most local sports or mountain shops. When tramping the back country, I recommend carrying a copy of *Moir's Guidebook* (New Zealand Alpine Club, 1977) or Burton and Atkinson's *Tramper's Guide To New Zealand's*

National Parks (Heinemann Reed, 1990).

The entire South Island can be fished using any New Zealand licence other than those of Rotorua and Taupo. It pays to be familiar with local rules and regulations as not all are printed on the licence. I have outlined some of these in this book, but changes may occur from year to year. If in doubt, please check with local fish and game councils or the Department of Conservation. There is no excuse for ignorance.

Finally, may the nor-wester blow as a gentle zephyr and the sun shine brightly on you. Good luck.

Safety and equipment

New Zealand is a narrow, mountainous, windy country with unpredictable weather patterns. It is frustrating to the fly fisher to carefully plan a day's fishing, then arrive to find that a howling downstream wind prevents any chance of casting. I have described the general direction each stream follows and strongly recommend you study the weather map and obtain a forecast before leaving for your day's fishing.

In the mountains, special care must be taken in planning routes, carrying survival equipment and informing others of your intentions. Do not attempt difficult river crossings, especially when the river is running high. Light a fire and camp out the night, miss a day or two at work but come home alive. Books are available on mountain safety, and accurate, detailed maps are essential. The following inventory has been developed during my many years of tramping and fishing New Zealand's back country.

Equipment for fishing and camping in the mountains

General gear
Small lightweight tent and fly. In summer, a fly alone or even a sheet of black polythene can be sufficient, but be prepared for sandflies and mosquitoes, especially on the West Coast. The tent should be insect proof.

Frame pack
Sleeping bag (preferably
  down)
Sleeping pad
Frypan
Knife (fishing or hunting)

Billies, 2
Pot-mitt
Cooker and fuel (fires can be
  lit in certain areas)
Fork, spoon, mug, plate
Torch (lightweight)

Matches (waterproof)
Piece of rubber or firelighters
Compass (optional)
Watch (can be used as a
  compass)
Fishing licence

Towel and toothbrush
First-aid kit
Soap (small piece)
Camera and film
Axe (lightweight)

Clothing

Boots (lightweight but must
  have commando-type sole
  for river crossings)
Underwear (one change)
Polypropylene T-shirt
Longs (lightweight but warm)

Socks (4 pairs)
Jersey (woollen)
Shorts
Sandshoes (to be kept dry)
Parka
Hat (with a brim)

Flannelette shirt or 'Swanndri' jacket with big pockets
Nylon overtrousers (excellent for wading with shorts as they
protect you from wind chill and sandflies and dry rapidly)

Fishing gear

Fly or spinning rod
  (preferably collapsible)
Reels and lines
Flies and/or spinners
Large plastic bag for fish

Traces
Polaroid glasses
Spring balance (for optimists!)
Scissors or nail-clippers
Day pack or pikau

Eel line (simple line and hook, great for survival)

Food

There's great scope for variety, but I choose from the following list.
Generally, trout, eel and occasionally venison (if a rifle is taken)
make welcome additions.

Bread (Vogel's or other
  wholegrain keeps longer)
Butter or margarine
Tea and coffee
Dried milk
Salt
Muesli
Scroggin (mixture of nuts,
  raisins, dried fruits, ginger,
  chocolate, etc.)

Brown sugar
Honey
Porridge
Bacon
Brown rice
Cheese
Salami
Freeze-dried meals in reserve
Packet soups
Dried vegetables

Equipment for a day's fishing

Clothing should be selected according to the season and area visited. I wear neutral colours to blend in with the background when fishing. Green, brown and blue are satisfactory, but yellow and red scare fish. Shiny varnish on a trout rod has the same effect. When fishing in boots and shorts, I use nylon overtrousers in cold or windy conditions; these also protect you from sandflies and keep stones out of your boots. On a warm day, I use anklets for this purpose. A shirt or fishing jacket with large, secure pockets is very useful. Do not forget a brimmed hat and polaroid glasses — essential for spotting fish. In a small day pack, or pikau, I carry lunch, matches, thermos, camera, fishing accessories, knife, plastic bags and spare clothing including a parka.

Fly fishing gear

Personal preference obviously governs your choice of rods, reels and flies. I prefer lightweight carbon-fibre rods, but fibreglass and split-cane rods are also satisfactory. On small streams some anglers are now using very light rods carrying weight-forward fly lines as light as No. 3 or No. 4. These are great providing conditions are ideal and the wind is behind you, but casting into a nor'wester on an exposed high-country lake becomes a problem with such fine gear. I use a general purpose 2.6 m carbon-fibre rod, a reel holding 60 m of backing and a weight-forward No. 6 line. There are two drums for this reel — one holding a floating line, the other a medium-sinking line. I carry Torture brand nylon of 2–3 kg breaking strain and an assortment of dry and wet flies, nymphs and lures. Occasionally, I make up tapered traces as they unroll easier when casting into a headwind.

A lightweight collapsible wide-mouthed landing net is very useful and also enables fish to be returned to the water with a minimum of handling. Remember to carry line float and silicon spray for dry flies. The choice of flies varies from district to district and from angler to angler, but I have listed popular patterns throughout the text. Visitors should spend time in sports stores and obtain as much local information as possible. However, it would certainly be useful to have a selection of the following in your fly box:

Caddis imitations

Caddis provides a large part of a trout's diet. Even in high summer, only 5 percent of trout food is taken from the surface. Early in the season, when rivers are full and trout are feeding on the bottom, it is difficult to present a true caddis imitation. Nymphs sufficiently weighted to sink to bottom-feeding fish are often much larger than the true imitation. However, a selection of weighted caddis nymphs and heavily weighted Hare and Copper nymphs should be carried. The adult caddis is represented by varieties of sedge patterns. I tie my own from deer hair. Small wet flies, such as Twilight Beauty, March Brown and Purple Grouse, fished on a floating line and greased leader are probably taken as a sedge and are certainly effective, especially after dusk.

Mayfly imitations
There are a wide variety of mayflies, which tend to vary from district to district, so local knowledge is useful. However, a selection of the following should be carried: Pheasant Tail, Half Back and Hare's Ear nymphs. Dad's Favourite, Twilight Beauty, Red Spinner and Kakahi Queen dry flies.

Beetle imitations
The manuka beetle can be represented by Coch-y-bondhu, Love's Lure and Royal Wulff dry flies.

Cicada imitations
Either a deer hair imitation or a large Coch-y-bondhu will suffice.

Willow grub and midge pupa imitations are difficult to find in sports stores, but both are occasionally useful. Black Gnat represents a blowfly and accounts for many back-country trout. In addition, large buoyant dry flies are very effective on rough back-country water. Patterns include Mole Fly, Palmer and Deer Hair. Just what they represent is another mystery that contributes to the fascination of fly fishing.

I always carry a few lures, such as small Rabbit patterns, Muddler Minnow and Parson's Glory for downstream fishing if the wind is strong, and for cruising lake trout. Parson's Glory and Rabbit flies are also good smelt patterns for sea-run fish. Remember your night lures, such as Mrs Simpson, Maribou, Hairy Dog, Fuzzy Wuzzy and Craig's Night-time.

Spin fishing gear

Rods

There are various lengths and weights of rod available in most sports shops. A 2–2.5 m fibreglass is recommended. A collapsible rod that will fit into a pack is an advantage. Some telescopic varieties fold to less than 0.5 m.

Reels

The old baitcasting reels controlled by your thumb have been superseded by the fixed spool reel with either open or closed face. The closed-face reel is ideal for beginners, but the casting distance is less than with the open-faced variety, which has a far greater line capacity and with which snarl-ups are easier to manage. To achieve maximum casting and retrieving capability, the drum should be filled to capacity with line.

Line

Monofilament line weights can vary, depending on conditions, from 1.5 to 4.5 kg.

Spinners

There are many varieties on the market, but a selection of Toby, Cobra, Flatfish, Penny, Tasmanian Devil, Billy Hill and Zed in different colours and weights is desirable. The smaller Veltic and Mepps spinners are useful in low-water summer conditions. The now-outdated Devons and other minnows such as Willesden Green, Eelskin and Brown Trout are still most effective, but efficient swivels are required to minimise line twist.

Boat fishing gear

Full safety equipment is essential when boat fishing. The larger lakes, such as Benmore, Wakatipu, Wanaka and Te Anau, can cut up rough even for sizeable craft. The same safety equipment required for coastal fishing should be taken on these lakes. This should include an auxiliary outboard, oars or paddles, flares, life-jackets, a tool-kit, anchor and warp and a bailer.

Fishing equipment can include boat or fly rods, reels and lines, flies and spinners, landing net, fish box and knife. A selection of Cobras, Tobys, Tasmanian Devils and Zed spinners should suffice.

If an auxiliary outboard is not used for trolling, boat speed can be reduced by towing a bucket or sack. When using lead line, remember that every 10 m (one colour) will sink 1–2 m. At the end of the lead line, attach 6–7 m of 6.5 kg nylon and then a 3 m-long trace with 4–5 kg breaking strain. This will enable fish to fight better, and if the line should snag, the lead line will not be lost. Remember to check rules and regulations regarding the use of lead or wire lines. If using monofilament line, a colour or two of lead line can be used to help it sink.

When trolling with a fly rod and a high-density fly line, let out all the line and 20–30 m of backing. Good trolling lures include Parson's Glory, Ginger Mick, Yellow Dorothy (Barred Rock), Rabbit patterns and Green Orbit in sizes 2 and 4. Generally, the most productive trolling can be obtained by following the blue line or drop-off. Remember, do not troll within 200 m of a stream mouth or shoreline angler.

Conservation

New Zealand anglers are indeed privileged. We have some of the highest quality angling for wild trout anywhere in the world. However, there is no room for complacency. Over the years, some New Zealand anglers have got used to feeding their families on trout. They regard trout as a source of food and the sport of catching them often takes second place. On Lakes Benmore and Taupo, I have seen anglers return with boatloads of fish; some even use home canning and bottling techniques to preserve their catch. With increasing pressure on fish resources from both local and overseas anglers, these days have surely passed. Many river fisheries are fragile environments and will not support the harvesting of large numbers of trout every season.

There seem to be three stages in the development of an angler. The novice will endeavour to catch as many fish as possible. Then comes the drive to catch the largest fish. Finally, the mature angler learns to appreciate the relationship between him- or herself and the environment and is quite content to release 90 percent of trout landed. Acclimatisation policy over recent years has been to allow most rivers to be self-sustaining, as overstocking often leads to fish migrating out to sea in search of food.

This doesn't mean that one or two fish cannot be taken for the table. Yet the bag limit in some districts — allowing, say, the taking of 10 or even 14 trout — is, I believe, totally ridiculous. Overstocking may be a problem in the Motueka River, but bag limits should be drastically reduced on most other streams. The bag limit on back-country rivers should be set at two fish. Overseas anglers have led the way with regard to catch and release and most Kiwi anglers are now practising such conservation measures. Briefly, this involves:

- The use of the strongest practical nylon tippets to facilitate quick landing of fish. Long playing leads to the buildup of harmful metabolites such as lactic acid, and this kills fish even after they appear to swim away unscathed.

- Care in handling fish. Use a wide-mouthed net to minimise handling. Wet the hands first, avoid the gill area, do not squeeze the stomach and take care not to rub off scales.
- The use of artery forceps or slim-jawed pliers for removing hooks.
- The use of barbless hooks. These are difficult to obtain but ordinary hooks can easily be 'adapted' by carefully snapping off the barb with slim-jawed pliers.

Anglers can assist fish and game councils and the Department of Conservation by weighing and measuring all trout taken and supplying details from their diaries at the end of each season. This is especially important for fish that have been marked or tagged. Tags should be returned, along with measurements, to the Department of Conservation. Metal or plastic tags are usually attached to the dorsal fin. Fish can also be marked by fin clipping or even removal. To determine right from left, look down on the fish's back with the head facing away from you. Always measure from the fork of the tail to the tip of the snout. Send details of species, weight, length, and time and area of capture. Angler co-operation is vital in managing a fishery.

In my opinion, more back-country areas, such as the beautiful Tasman Wilderness Area in the North-west Nelson Forest Park, should be set aside as wilderness zones, where helicopters are prohibited. Anglers keen and fit enough to seek out trophy fish would then face a real challenge. Helicopters have their place and I have used them to my advantage in the past. But it can be depressing to have a machine land upstream from where you are fishing after you have spent three days tramping into an isolated spot, and to watch a well-dressed angler step out to fish the pool immediately above you.

Anglers should always extend courtesy to landowners. Few farmers will deny access to fishing water provided permission is sought first. Please shut gates, avoid disturbing stock and offer thanks on the way out. Remember, the cost of fishing in many other countries is well out of reach for most anglers. Fortunately we have not yet reached that stage in New Zealand, but treat landowners with respect so access for others will not be denied. Most anglers I have met really care for the environment, but please remove your rubbish and do not light fires indiscriminately. Fish should be cleaned well away from the river or lake edge, fish guts deeply buried and not discarded into the waterway.

A number of rivers have deteriorated over the years as a result of clear-felling the banks, irrigation and other farming operations. Many farmers I have spoken to are totally unaware of the factors that lead to a deterioration in water quality. Catchment operations, shingle removal, land drainage and river straightening have all seriously affected some waterways. It's a mystery why some local authorities have spent so much time and money straightening rivers in order to minimise flooding rather than replanting the banks and headwaters.

In New Zealand we pride ourselves on our clean air and unpolluted rivers and lakes. Without doubt, the best fishing rivers tend to rise in undeveloped country clothed in native bush. In order to protect existing rivers and improve others it is essential that stock be fenced off and a buffer zone established along each bank. Scrub and bank vegetation will then slow erosion, reduce fertiliser leaching into the water, provide trout food and improve habitat.

Unfortunately, fencing is costly but the long-term benefits obtained by improving water quality far outweigh these costs. No one will deny that controlled irrigation is essential for some farming operations and shingle removal necessary for roading, but one only needs to look at the many polluted waterways in Europe and the United States to appreciate that New Zealand has a priceless asset to preserve, both for recreation and tourism. Anglers have a duty to care for their rivers and lakes that provide so much pleasure, and can exert considerable political pressure to promote their protection.

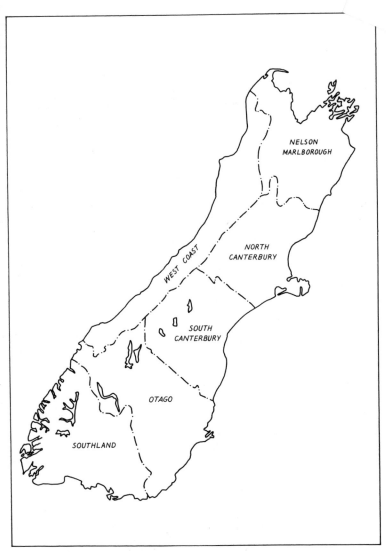

South Island Fish and Game Council Districts

Nelson-Marlborough District

This district offers a wide variety of exciting brown trout fishing. There are two mountain lakes in the Nelson Lakes National Park, a hydro lake and a variety of snow-fed and rain-fed rivers in the Nelson area. Two main river systems dominate the Waimea Plains lying between the North-west Nelson Forest Park to the west, the Richmond Range to the east and the Nelson Lakes National Park to the south. These are the Motueka and Waimea rivers which flow gently across alluvial farm and orchard land. Marlborough is generally hilly and occupies the north-east corner of the South Island. The prevailing westerly winds and high mountain ranges in the interior create a warm, dry climate in summer and a frosty, cool climate in winter.

Trout and salmon were first liberated in the Marlborough rivers about 1876 by the Marlborough Acclimatisation Society. While trout have thrived, the quinnat salmon found the sea temperature too high and have not done well, though there is still a small run of salmon up the Wairau River in the autumn. There are two worthwhile river systems to fish — the Wairau and the Pelorus. Hydro-electric stations have been built on the Waihopi and Branch rivers, both Wairau tributaries, but neither has an adverse effect on the fishery.

Unless otherwise specified, the season opens on 1 October and closes on 30 April and the bag limit is four trout. Ten trout is the bag limit on the Aorere River, the Motueka River below the Wangapeka confluence, the Buller River below the Gowan confluence, Lakes Rotoiti and Rotorua, the Cobb Reservoir, and the Maruia and Matakitaki rivers. Minimum size is 30 cm.

Paturau River
This river drains the bush-clad Wakamarama Range and enters the sea at Paturau, south of Cape Farewell. It's a medium to small shingly river and, though not highly recommended, it does hold brown trout, but it's very isolated and only worth fishing if visiting this scenic part of the west coast.

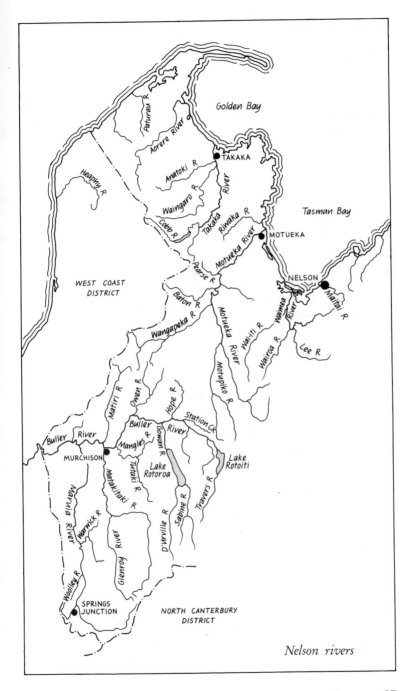

Paturau R.

Aorere River

Golden Bay

Anatoki R

TAKAKA

Heaphy R

Waingaro R

Cobb R

Takaka River

Riwaka R

Takaka River

Tasman Bay

Motueka River

MOTUEKA

Pearse R

WEST COAST
DISTRICT

NELSON

Maitai R

Baron R

Motueka River

Wai-iti R

Waimea River

Wangapeka R

Wairoa R

Lee R

Motupiko R

Matiri R

Owen R

Hope R

Buller River

Station Ck

Buller River

Goswell R

Mangles R

Lake
Rotoroa

Lake
Rotoiti

MURCHISON

Tintaki R

Marvila River

Matakitaki R

D'Urville R

Sabine R

Travers R

Warwick R

Glenroy River

Woolley R

SPRINGS
JUNCTION

NORTH CANTERBURY
DISTRICT

Nelson rivers

Aorere River

Location   Lies in the west of the Nelson district. Flows north-east, draining the Tasman Mountains, Wakamarama and Haupiri ranges, and enters Golden Bay at Collingwood.

Access   From S.H.60 to Collingwood, roads follow upriver to Rockville, Bainham and Brown Hut at the start of the Heaphy Track.

Season   1 October–30 April. Below the roadbridge at Rockville, it is open season all year.

This is a good brown trout river, holding fish averaging around 1.5 kg with larger fish in the inaccessible headwaters. Although fishing can be patchy at times, drift dives have revealed good stocks of brown trout (50 fish/km at Devils Boot). Fish can be readily spotted and stalked in the middle and upper reaches and the river is wadable. An active evening rise occurs in favourable conditions. The upper reaches flow through rugged bush country, but for the energetic angler, there is always the chance of a trophy fish. A 2- to 3-hour track from Brown Hut to Shakespeare Flat leads to good remote fishing. Spinning accounts for most trout caught in this river.

There are a few trout in the remote, peat-stained Heaphy River, but this is mainly of interest to trampers walking the Heaphy Track either from Bainham or Karamea and is not worth a special visit.

Cobb River

Location   The Cobb River drains Lake Cobb and the Lockett and Peel ranges, flows south-east, and enters the Cobb Reservoir formed when the Cobb River was dammed for hydro-electric power. Below the Reservoir, the Cobb joins the Takaka River below the Cobb powerhouse.

Access   From Upper Takaka, turn off at the Rat Trap Hotel and take the Cobb Dam road up the valley. This follows the south-eastern shore of the reservoir to Myttons car-park and the Trilobite Hut at the head of the reservoir.

Restrictions   Fly fishing only is permitted upstream from the first gorge above the Cobb Reservoir.

There's a Department of Conservation office on the ridge above the Cobb Reservoir, where information about the Cobb Valley can be obtained.

The most enjoyable fishing is in the river at the head of the reservoir above Trilobite Hut, where there are mainly rainbow trout which can easily be spotted in clear runs and pools. The valley, confined between bush-covered hills with the river winding across tussock flats and through patches of beech bush, is very attractive.

Cobb Reservoir
(See the Cobb River, above, for location and access.)

This rather shallow hydro lake is open for fishing all year round and contains brown and rainbow trout averaging around 1 kg. Best fished with a spinner, either trolling from a boat or threadlining from the shore. In bright conditions the occasional cruising fish can be stalked from the shore. Boat-launching facilities are available. Junior anglers fish this reservoir with live bait.

Takaka River

Location and access   Drains the Arthur Range and joins the Cobb River at the powerhouse, then flows for 8 km through steep, bush-clad country with the road some distance above the river, which emerges from these hills to flow placidly across farmland in a northerly direction to Takaka and enter Golden Bay north of this township. The road from Takaka to Upper Takaka and the Cobb Reservoir follows the river, though in the upper reaches it runs well above the river.

The most exciting fishing lies in the gorge upstream from where the Cobb Reservoir road crosses the river. There are well-defined pools and runs for 8 km upstream from the bridge to the powerhouse and the Cobb River confluence. The true right bank is bush covered, and boots and shorts are advised as a considerable amount of scrambling is required. The Takaka holds good-sized browns easily seen in the clear water. In the middle and lower reaches spinning during the day accounts for most fish. Lure fishing after dark with a large night lure fished deep through the holes under the willows is also popular. There are a few sea-run fish in the lower reaches early in the season.

Both the Waingaro and Anatoki tributaries, which join the true left bank of the Takaka River upstream from Takaka, hold trout but are not highly recommended. The Anatoki is well known for its tame eels.

Riwaka River

Location   The north branch emerges from an impressive, deep, dark-blue spring on the Takaka Hill south of Riwaka township. The main stream flows north-east through farmland and enters Tasman Bay near Riwaka just west of Motueka.

Access   The scenic Riwaka River Valley road leaves S.H.60 a few kilometres west of Riwaka township at the foot of the Takaka Hill and follows up the true left bank. It is a short scramble to the stream.

Restrictions   Fly fishing only. Catch and release recommended.

This small, clear, shingly stream is overhung by willows and vegetation in places but is a delight to fish and holds good stocks of brown trout in the 0.5–1.2 kg range. Drift dives have revealed good stocks of takable fish in the river near the Moss Bush picnic area. Use the same flies as for the Motueka River. There are some great picnic spots, and it's well worth visiting for fly anglers, offering easy access and safe wading, though the stones are slippery. Fish are not easy to spot against the brown stones.

The popular Motueka River offers long glides and deep holding pools.

Motueka River and tributaries

Motueka River

> **Location**   Drains the Richmond Range to the east, the Hope and Lookout ranges to the south and the Arthur Range to the west. Flows in a northerly direction from the Motupiko–Tadmor districts through Ngatimoti to enter Tasman Bay just north of Motueka.
>
> **Access**   The river is well serviced with roads on both sides of the river from the Golden Downs Forest to its mouth near Motueka some 60 km away. S.H.61 follows the river upstream on the east bank from Motueka to S.H.6 at Kohatu. There are a number of public accesses and the river can also be approached across private farmland providing prior permission is obtained.
>
> **Season**   Downstream from the roadbridge at Alexander Bluff the river is open all year. Elsewhere, 1 October–30 April.
>
> **Restrictions**   The bag limit below the confluence with the Wangapeka is 10 trout. Elsewhere, 4 trout.

Despite being very popular and heavily fished this river holds an abundance of brown trout averaging around 1 kg although fish up to 2.5 kg are occasionally taken. Fish stocks equal any other river in New Zealand (275 fish/km at Woodstock). The river is wide and offers long glides and ripples flowing over a stable shingle bed which can be easily waded in most areas. There are also some very deep holding pools. The banks are willow lined but present no great obstruction to casting. Fish can be spotted in some areas but the fish population is so high that any pool or run is likely to hold fish and can therefore be fished blind.

During the day try a small (sizes 16–18) Coch-y-bondhu, Adams, Dad's Favourite or Molefly. Any small, lightly weighted nymph is effective in the shallow water, while a heavier nymph should be tried for the deeper runs. There's a good evening rise during summer and fish respond to mayfly imitations such as Kakahi Queen and Twilight Beauty in sizes 14–16. At dusk I have had success with a small dark sedge or a small sparsely tied wet fly such as Twilight Beauty, Purple Grouse, Alder or March Brown fished either upstream or across and swung with the current on a floating line. Fish tend to take these flies just when they start to speed up on the swing. Sensitivity is called for with this method as unless the line is tightened immediately a fish takes, the deception will be quickly rejected. This is a great river for the angler learning the art of fly fishing.

The spin angler should use a small Veltic, a gold or silver Toby, or a Meps and fish the deeper runs under the willows. As is usually the case, fishing with a spinner is better after a fresh.

There's a good camping ground at Alexander Bluff's Bridge 10 km south of Motueka, and one can spend a very enjoyable holiday on this river during the warm Nelson summers.

Motupiko River

> **Location** Drains the St Arnaud Range and flows north to join the Motueka at Kohatu.
>
> **Access** S.H.6 follows this river upstream from Kohatu, but a short walk across private farmland is sometimes necessary to reach the river. Public access is available at Quinneys Bush Reserve and the Tunnicliffe and Korere bridges.

This is a spawning tributary which joins the Motueka at Kohatu and is reserved for fly fishing only. The river is similar in character to the Motueka but smaller. It tends to fish better early and late in the season as hot summers and reduced water flows often force fish back into the main river. The best fishing is in the first 5 km above the Motueka confluence. There are only a few fish above this. Fish can easily be spotted, especially in the deeper runs against the cliffs, but are just as easily frightened, and respond to the same fly methods as for the parent river. Catch and release is strongly recommended as stocks are not high.

Wangapeka River

> **Location** Drains the Herbert Range of the North-west Nelson Forest Park, flows in a northerly direction and enters the Motueka River 7 km downstream from Tapawera.
>
> **Access** From Tapawera on S.H.61 take the road to Tadmor and Matariki, then follow the Wangapeka River road. This road follows the river upstream, but do not take your vehicle beyond the Dart Ford unless the weather is settled or you have a four-wheel-drive. Access to the middle and lower reaches is generally across private farmland, but permission is seldom refused to a considerate angler.

The Wangapeka Track follows this river up to the Karamea and Little Wanganui headwaters, a route popular with trampers. In the upper reaches, the banks are bush covered; the middle and lower reaches wind through bracken-covered hills and across farmland. The banks are stable and there are some pleasant pools and runs, but the river discolours easily in a fresh. Fish can be spotted and stalked, especially in the upper reaches, and the brown trout respond in similar fashion to their relatives in the Motueka. To those willing to tramp, fish up to 2.5 kg have been taken in the upper reaches.

The Baton and Pearse tributaries joining the true left bank of the Motueka River near Woodstock used to be favoured 30 years ago, but because of their instability during a fresh, fishing has been patchy. However, recent drift dives have revealed a reasonable number of fish in the Baton, especially above the gorge (50 fish/km above the concrete ford). Fish can be spotted in this clear stream draining the Arthur Range. An old schoolteacher of mine told me of great days he had spent on the Baton with a small, very basic ginger-hackled dry fly. To avoid the usual congestion of feather, silk and glue at the head of the fly, the hackle was tied in down the shank of the hook and plenty of room left for the head.

There are great picnic spots under beech trees in the Baton Valley. Both these tributaries fish better either early or late in the season. The Pearse is reserved for fly fishing only.

Waimea River

Location The Wairoa and Wai-iti tributaries join to form the Waimea River near Brightwater.
Access S.H.60 crosses the lower tidal reaches near Appleby and gives access to a camping reserve, while S.H.6 crosses at Brightwater some 7 km upstream. Blackbyre Road follows the river's east bank from S.H.60 to S.H.6. Clover and Haycocks roads lead to Max's Bush picnic reserve in the upper reaches.

This willow-lined river with a shingle bed is similar in character to the Motueka River. There are long glides and shallow runs. Despite the riverbed's being rather unstable, there are reasonable numbers of brown trout in the 0.5–0.75 kg range which can be taken on flies or spinners, but fish are difficult to spot. The lower reaches occasionally produce large sea-run fish which are usually caught in deep holes at night on a sunk black lure such as a Mrs Simpson, Hairy Dog or Fuzzy Wuzzy.

The Wairoa Gorge road leads to great swimming holes and though I have seldom bothered to fish there, drift dives have revealed a surprisingly high number of fish in the gorge area. The smaller tributaries of the Wairoa hold a few fish but are not recommended.

The Maitai Stream in Nelson City holds small brown trout and is great for junior anglers. It is reserved for fly fishing only. The Wakapuaka River, crossed by S.H.6 at Hira on the Nelson side of the Whangamoa Saddle, also holds small brown trout and is quite heavily fished by local anglers. Access is off the road to Cable Bay. It is not worth a special visit.

Rai River

Location and access   This small tributary of the Pelorus River joins the main stream at Pelorus Bridge. S.H.75, running parallel to this stream for 10 km in the Rai Valley above the falls, provides easy access across farmland.

Restrictions   Fly fishing only in this stream. The bag limit is 2 fish.

The Rai River – highly recommended to the 'purist.'

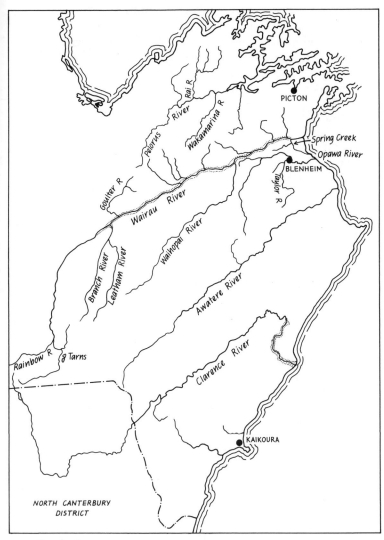

Marlborough rivers

This excellent small stream flowing across farmland is lined by bush and willows and holds very high stocks of small to medium-sized brown and rainbow trout (200 fish/km above the falls). These can be spotted in ideal conditions and will accept small nymphs and dry flies carefully presented on fine gear. Trout may be seen scattering in all directions if one doesn't approach the stream with care. It's not an easy stream to fish because of long, clear glides and bank obstruction, but wading is generally unnecessary except to cross the stream. Fishing is best early in the season as farming effluent and low waterflows in summer can cause eutrophication problems. The Rai is highly recommended to the 'purist'.

Pelorus River

Location   Drains the Richmond Range and flows in a northerly direction through the Mt Richmond State Forest Park and Canvastown before entering Pelorus Sound at Havelock.

Access   S.H.6 follows the river upstream from Havelock to the popular overnight camping and picnic ground at Pelorus Bridge. Private farmland must be crossed. The metalled Mangatapu Valley road continues upstream for 13 km on the true left bank from Pelorus Bridge. From the road end at Larges Clearing, a well-marked tramping track continues to Captain Creek and Middy huts. Middy Hut is six hours' tramp from the road end and there is little fishing beyond this point.

The Pelorus contains a good stock of mainly brown trout in the 1–1.5 kg range though there are a few rainbow, mainly in the lower reaches. Larger fish are found in the upper reaches if one is prepared to tramp, but numbers are not high. The river has a stable rock and shingle bed with deep, clear holes in the upper reaches and long glides and shallow runs in the middle and lower reaches. The upper reaches flow through native bush, while below Pelorus Bridge the banks are lined with willows, poplars and clumps of manuka.

Fish can be spotted, especially above Pelorus Bridge, but tend to be shy. The river is easily waded below Pelorus Bridge where there's a good stock of fish and an active evening rise in summer. The river is tidal a few kilometres below Canvastown, and between here and Pelorus Bridge access is generally across private farmland. Fish respond during the day to weighted Pheasant Tail nymphs or a small Kakahi Queen or Coch-y-bondhu dry fly in sizes 14–16. For the evening rise try a Twilight Beauty dry fly. If fish ignore dry flies during the rise, try a small wet fly such as Purple Grouse, Bradshaw's Fancy or March Brown fished across and down with the current on a floating line. This river is highly recommended for the fly fisher. At night there are numerous small eels in the shallows.

The Wakamarina River, entering the Pelorus River at Canvastown, holds a few fish but is mainly fished by trampers walking the Wakamarina Track.

Wairau River and tributaries

Wairau River

Location　This large, snow-fed river drains the St Arnaud Range and flows north-east to enter Cloudy Bay near Blenheim.

Access　The upper reaches can be reached from S.H.63 by following the private Hanmer Springs hydro road through Rainbow Station. Permission must be obtained from the station owner as there is a locked gate. This road leads eventually to Hanmer but is often closed by snow after Easter. Four-wheel-drive vehicles have a distinct advantage as the road can be rough in parts. S.H.63 follows the river from Rainbow Station downstream to Renwick. S.H.6 crosses the river at Renwick while S.H.1 crosses the lower reaches near Spring Creek.

Season　Winter extension below the Wash Bridge and in the Diversion Channel from 1 May to 31 August. Elsewhere, 1 October–30 April.

Restrictions　The bag limit above the Wash Bridge is 4 trout only.

This magnificent river has more than 100 km of fishable water. The middle and lower reaches tend to be unstable and braided on a shingle bed and are more suited to spinning. However, there are some deep holes containing good fish, especially when whitebait are running. Try a smelt fly during the day or a deeply sunk black lure at night in the holes.

Above Rainbow Station the river is more confined and stable on a rock and stone bed. There's excellent water for 15 km above the locked gate at Six Mile Creek. Brown trout up to 4.5 kg can be stalked, but they are not easy to see in the heavy water as they rise quickly in the current to inspect a fly and then disappear just as rapidly into the green depths. It's often an advantage to have a mate spotting from the bank above the river.

Fish respond to well-weighted nymphs and occasionally to large buoyant dry flies, such as deer hair patterns and Mole Fly or Palmer varieties. Don't be discouraged if your nymph is at first refused. I watched a very competent angler continue to cast over a large fish until it eventually took the deception on about the forty-eighth cast. Maybe it was asleep!

The water is rather heavy and the river is best fished in boots and shorts. Wading can be tricky and crossings downright hazardous in parts. Hot spots are at Dip Flat and Irishman Flat although fish can be taken anywhere in this area. The reaches of the Wairau above the Rainbow confluence are worth fishing, and for the energetic angler prepared to tramp, the Rainbow itself, and the Begely tributary, hold a few fish, but there are spawning streams for the main river. An occasional salmon also runs up this far late in the season.

Two of the Wairau's tributaries, the Rainbow and the Begely, are briefly mentioned above.

The Branch and the Leatham

Location and access   Both flow in a northerly direction to join the true right bank of the Wairau at the Branch some 70 km upriver from Blenheim on S.H.63. A small side road gives access to both rivers.

These unstable rivers, which drain high tussock country on private property, are prone to flash floods. In addition, a hydro-electric station has recently been built on the Branch just above its confluence with the Wairau, though this does not affect the fishing. The Leatham is the more stable as the upper reaches flow through patches of native bush. There are a few fish in these upper reaches if one is prepared to combine tramping with fishing, but stocks are not high.

Goulter River

Location and access   This highly rated tributary drains Lake Chalice and enters the Wairau upstream from the end of North Bank Road. Cross the Wairau at Renwick and follow this road upstream to the car-park at Patriarch. There's a rough farm track through the Patriarch Station to the river. Please ask permission.

If one is prepared to walk excellent brown trout fishing is available from this scenic bush-lined river. It's by far the best tributary of the

Wairau and water flows remain consistent throughout summer. The Mid Goulter Hut, 6 km upstream on a track following the true left bank, is an ideal base. The river is stable, the countryside most attractive, and good fish can be spotted in clear pools and runs. Catch and release is advocated.

Note: Lake Chalice contains native trout only.

Opawa River

Location and access   Flows through the outskirts of Blenheim before joining the Wairau near its mouth. S.H.1 crosses north of Blenheim while Thomsons Ford and Hammerichs roads lead to the river further upstream.

Season   Below S.H.1, 1 October–31 August. Elsewhere, 1 October–30 April.

This small, clear stream containing very shy brown trout is popular with junior anglers. Small nymphs or a sunk night lure take most fish. It's best early in the season before weed chokes the river.

A tributary of the Opawa River, the Taylor River, flowing through Blenheim, also holds small brown trout and is fished by the local lads.

Spring Creek

Location and access   Crossed by S.H.1 near Spring Creek 5 km north of Blenheim. Access also off O'Dwyers and Rapaura roads west of Spring Creek, but permission must be obtained before crossing private farmland.

This gin-clear, narrow, deep, weedy, spring-fed stream holds excellent stocks of good-sized browns and offers fly fishers a real challenge. Flowing across farmland, with grassy and willow-lined banks, this stream can rise after rain but generally remains clear. It's highly regarded by fly fishers, and drift dives have revealed excellent stocks of large fish (25 large browns per kilometre), but they are hard to catch, often hiding beneath the banks and weed beds only to emerge at night to feed.

During the day, try small dry flies (sizes 16–18) such as Dad's Favourite, Adams, Greenwell's Glory and Twilight Beauty or small weighted nymphs of the Caddis variety, Pheasant Tail or Half Back. A sunk black lure slowly retrieved at night can bring results. Weed and snags also affect the catch rate and fish will only succumb to the experienced angler. Some overseas anglers return each year to fish this creek, such is its popularity.

The Awatere and Clarence rivers, crossed by S.H.1 at Seddon and north of Kaikoura respectively, are not worth visiting. They are unstable and usually silt-laden, though there are a few fish in the deeper holes. Try a spinner if desperate. The upper reaches of the Clarence are very different, and well worth fishing. They are described in the North Canterbury section.

The Tarns at Tarndale

> **Location**   Headwaters of the Wairau on Tarndale.
>
> **Access**   By permission of Molesworth and Rainbow stations and a walk off the private hydro road. (See map.)

These tarns, lying in exposed swampy tussock country, hold brown trout averaging 1.4 kg with an occasional fish up to 3 kg. Sedgemere Lake covers one hectare and is only a 50 m walk from the end of the vehicle track; Island Lake, covering 1.5 ha, is 15 minutes' walk from the end of the vehicle track, while Bowscale Lake covers 2 ha and is an hour's walk from a marked gate at the end of the vehicle track.

There are other unnamed tarns in the area also holding fish. Wind is the main problem for the fly fisher, but in bright, calm conditions cruising fish can be spotted and fished for with a dry fly such as a Black Gnat, Red Palmer, Coch-y-bondhu and Mole Fly. They also respond to a lightly weighted nymph or lure of the bully type, such as Lord's Killer or Muddler Minnow, cast well ahead of a cruising fish. Weed beds can make it difficult for threadlining. Sedgemere Lake and Island Lake are both stocked from small tributaries of the Alma River, which joins the upper reaches of the Acheron River. Fish Lake connects with the Wairau River.

Nelson Lakes National Park

The Park covers 100 470 ha of rugged mountains and unspoilt native bush, and contains two major lakes and a number of exciting rivers. Sufficient snow falls in winter to provide skiing on Mt Robert, but summer temperatures warm the lakes for swimming and boating.

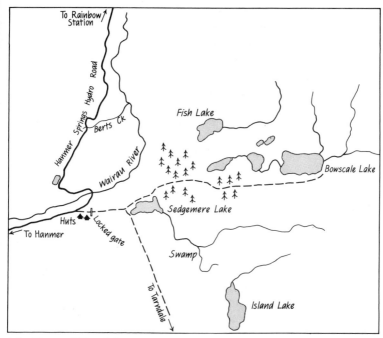

The Tarns of Tarndale

Visitors to the Park should visit the Park Headquarters at St Arnaud for maps and general information. There are motel and camping facilities available at both lakes. Insect repellent for sandflies is recommended!

Lake Rotoiti

Location and access   Turn off S.H.6, from Nelson to Murchison, at Kawatiri Junction onto S.H.63. It's 25 km to the lake, which can also be reached from the Wairau Valley and Tophouse.

Season   Open all year except for September.

Restrictions   The bag limit is 10 trout. Trolling is prohibited within 200 m of stream inlets and the outlet.

Boat-launching facilities   At St Arnaud on the northern shore.

This mountain lake is fed by melting snow water from the Travers River at the head of the lake and drained by the Buller River at the outlet. The lake, which is surrounded by bush, covers 1 100 ha, is 9 km long and lies at an altitude of 600 m. It contains brown trout averaging around 1–1.5 kg, and is best fished from a boat, either harling a Parson's Glory, Rabbit pattern or Muddler Minnow on a deep sinking line or trolling a spinner such as a Toby or Cobra.

Fly casting with a small sunk lure or dry fly is generally restricted to a boat. Exceptions are at the mouth of the Travers River at the southern end of the lake and at the outlet and start of the Buller River. Fish will rise here on warm, calm summer evenings. The odd cruising fish can be spotted around the shore. Try a Green Beetle imitation for these.

Travers River

Location and access Drains Mt Travers (2 338 m) and surrounding peaks and flows in a northerly direction down a very scenic valley to enter the head or southern end of Lake Rotoiti. There are well-marked tramping tracks through the bush round both sides of the lake, but the journey may take 3–4 hours. This time can be considerably shortened by hiring a boat to the Lakehead or Coldwater huts at the head of the lake.

The Upper Buller River, a highly regarded, self-sustaining brown trout fishery.

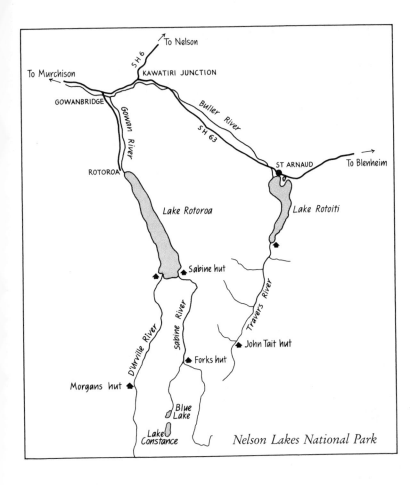

To Nelson

SH 6

KAWATIRI JUNCTION

To Murchison

GOWANBRIDGE

Gowan River

Buller River

SH 63

ROTOROA

ST ARNAUD

To Blenheim

Lake Rotoroa

Lake Rotoiti

Sabine hut

Travers River

Sabine River

D'Urville River

John Tait hut

Forks hut

Morgans hut

Blue Lake

Lake Constance

Nelson Lakes National Park

This valley is worth visiting for the scenery alone as the river winds across wide tussock flats edged with beech bush. The river has a reasonably stable shingle bed and holds brown trout averaging 1 kg which can be spotted and stalked in very clear water all the way upstream to the John Tait Hut, but you will be disturbed by trampers in summer. Try Coch-y-bondhu, Palmer varieties, Mole Fly and Twilight Beauty dry flies, Hare and Copper, Pheasant Tail and Half Back nymphs, all in sizes 12–16. The 10 km of fishable water is best fished on hot days from December to March when visibility is good.

Cattle used to graze this valley; as a teenager, I once had the mortification of arriving back at my campsite after a day's fishing to find a steer standing with one foot through my pup tent!

Buller River (upper reaches)

Location   Drains Lake Rotoiti, flows west to Kawatiri Junction then turns and flows south to Murchison. Below the inaccessible Upper Buller Gorge at Lyell, the river enters the West Coast district.

Access   S.H.6 follows the river upstream from Murchison to Kawatiri Junction; S.H.63 follows the river to Lake Rotoiti. There are many access points for anglers off these roads, although a considerable walk across farmland is sometimes needed to reach the river. Below Kawatiri Junction easy access is only available at picnic spots and at the Murchison camping ground.

Restrictions   The bag limit below the confluence with the Gowan is 10 fish. Above this point, 4 fish.

This highly regarded self-sustaining brown trout fishery holds fish averaging 1.5 kg. Below the confluence with the Gowan, the Buller becomes a large river with heavy water and except in selected spots is more suited to spinning. The river is stable with a rock and stone bed. The stretch upstream from Kawatiri Junction offers excellent fly fishing, the best water being the first 5 km below the outlet where fish stocks are very high.

Fish can be spotted by the observant angler, although many will be missed in the rougher sections of the river. The brown stones also provide excellent camouflage. In places the river is swift, overgrown and difficult to fish but trout frequent these pockets of rough water and fight vigorously when hooked. During low water conditions the river can be crossed, in selected fords, in boots and shorts, but use a manuka pole for stability as the stones are very slippery.

Trout respond to heavily weighted nymphs such as Hare and Copper, Half Back and Green Stonefly; in the fast runs use sizes 8–10. A well-hackled dry fly with good flotation features, such as a bivisible deer hair pattern, in sizes 10–12, is equally well accepted.

The upper reaches remain clear even after a fresh. Around Murchison there is often a vigorous sedge rise on warm summer evenings. Try a small wet fly on a floating line fished across and down or a sedge pattern tied on a size 10 hook.

Lake Rotoroa

This lake, at 20 km long and 2 km wide, is both longer and larger than Lake Rotoiti. Surrounded by dense native bush and mountain

ranges, it is very attractive. The Sabine and D'Urville rivers enter the
top or southern end of the lake while a major tributary of the Buller
River, the Gowan, drains the northern end. A ranger station offers
information along with camping and motel facilities. The sandflies
can be vicious, so take insect repellent.

The lake can best be fished from a boat, either trolling, harling
or casting on the drift as on Lake Rotoiti. Both rainbow and brown
trout are found averaging 1.3 kg. Hot spots are the deltas of the Sabine
and D'Urville rivers and the outlet. There's a marked track along the
eastern shore to the lakehead, but as this takes approximately 5–6 hours
to tramp most visitors use a boat. This can be easily arranged. For
many years the guest house and boat service were run by the Flowers
brothers, delightful characters known locally as 'Daff and Dil'.

Sabine River

The river holds brown and rainbow trout with an occasional fish up
to 3 kg. Upstream from the Sabine Hut near the head of the lake
there is an unfishable gorge holding a few very large fish. There is
good fishable rock and stone mountain stream water all the way to
the Forks Hut. Fish can be spotted in the slower pools, but in summer
don't neglect the rough, boisterous, well-oxygenated stretches, which
often hold trout. Lake Constance and the Blue Lake on the west branch
are worth a visit for the tramper, but purely for the scenery as they
do not hold trout.

D'Urville River

Location and access   The D'Urville mouth and D'Urville Hut can be reached by walking round the lake edge from the wharf at the Sabine Hut.

The D'Urville flows in a bush-covered scenic valley parallel to, but west of, the Sabine. In contrast, this river holds mainly brown trout. It is best fished early and late in the season as reduced water flows can force fish back to the lake in dry summer conditions. Trout are easily spotted in bright conditions. There is 12 km of fishable water to well above Morgans Hut. Use the same flies as for the Travers.

Gowan River

Location   Drains Lake Rotoroa and flows north-west for 11 km before joining the Buller River.

Access   The Gowan Valley road generally follows the river, although access is often impeded by native bush and steep banks covered in blackberry, bracken and willow. Permission should be obtained before crossing private farmland.

This is a swift-flowing, clear, boisterous river and only fit anglers in boots and shorts should attempt to fish it. The riverbed is weedy and the rocks very slippery to wade across. Clear stretches for fly casting are limited. Similar methods to those described for the Buller should be used, with the addition of downstream lure fishing with a Muddler Minnow or Rabbit fly on a fast-sinking line. Both rainbow and brown trout are present and are generally in excellent condition. Drift dives have revealed a very high trout population in this river (350 fish/km at the outlet), but most lie deep and shelter from the strong current behind large boulders.

There are certainly trout in this river, but the fishing is difficult. It's important to use heavily weighted nymphs in sizes 8–12 in order to get down to the fish in the fast water. A sink-tipped line is an advantage and it may even be worth trying the Tongariro method – using two weighted nymphs tied 10–20 cm apart. A large deer-hair dry fly that floats well can also be effective. An occasional fish can be spotted, but the white water should be fished blind with a well-weighted nymph, though landing a fish is another matter. It's not easy to follow a good-conditioned fish downstream so at least a

4 kg leader should be used. There are few beaches where one can land a fish so carry a landing net. Like the Upper Buller River, the Gowan remains fishable after heavy rain, but the current becomes even stronger.

Owen River

Location and access   This small, gentle stream flows in a southerly direction from the Lookout Range and Mt Owen to join the Buller at Owen River Junction on S.H.6 a few kilometres south of Gowan Bridge. The Owen Valley road follows the river upstream for 12 km on the true left bank, but access to the river is difficult in places because of blackberry, scrub, bracken and willows. The riverbed is easy to negotiate.

The Owen is a delightful stream to fish although trout stocks are not high. Water tends to be brownish in colour, but trout can be spotted. The river is easy to wade and cross. A few years ago our family dined on trout stuffed with mushrooms and fresh blackberries all collected from the Owen Valley. It is best fished early in the season; catch and release recommended.

Mangles River

Location   Rises in the bush-clad Braeburn Range. The Tiraumea and Tutaki tributaries join at Tutaki to form the Mangles, while the Blackwater joins lower down. This small river flows in a westerly direction to join the Buller at Longford, a few kilometres north of Murchison on S.H.6.

Access   The Tutaki Valley road leaves S.H.6 5 km north of Murchison at Longford and follows the river to Tutaki.

Restrictions   Fly fishing only. The bag limit is 4 trout.

This delightful stream, holding good stocks of brown trout averaging 1 kg (130 fish/km in the gorge), is highly recommended. Fish are not easy to spot in the lower reaches or gorge where the river is overgrown in places with beech bush, scrub and blackberry and the water boisterous and greenish in colour. There are also some very deep holes. However, 10 km upstream the river flows across farmland and is more sedate, with well-developed pools and riffles.

Fish respond to most weighted nymphs in sizes 12–16. There's often

The exquisite Mangles River is a delight to fish.

a good evening rise on this stream, but watch for fish nymphing and breaking the surface rather than rising. The river can be waded, even through the gorge, but the riverbed is slippery. Catch and release is recommended. Please ask for permission to cross private farmland.

The Tutaki River holds some good fish, especially early and late in the season, but can become silt laden after rain and warm in low-water summer conditions.

Matiri River

Location and access   Drains the Matiri Range, flows in a southerly direction and enters the Buller River just west of Murchison. The Matiri Valley road follows the river upstream from the Longford Bridge north of Murchison.

Another small stream holding brown trout in the 0.75–1 kg range, this stream was blocked by a landslide during the Murchison earthquake in 1929 and a small lake, Lake Matiri, was created. The fishing in this stream is only average, and a recently proposed hydro-electric power station, if built, will further reduce the resource. Lake Matiri holds browns but is not recommended.

Matakitaki River

Location and access   Drains the Spenser Mountains and generally follows a north-westerly course to join the Buller just south of Murchison. The road to Matakitaki from Murchison generally follows the river upstream although at times it's some distance away across private land. The upper reaches can be reached via the Mangles–Tutaki Valley road through Tutaki to the Matakitaki Station. Secure permission before tramping up the valley.

Restrictions   The bag limit is 10 fish.

There are only a few fish in deep pools in the headwaters around Downie Hut. Below this point and as far downstream as Upper Matakitaki, the river tends to be large, shingly and unstable during floods. At Matakitaki, the river is more confined and flows through beech bush and farmland with an occasional gorgy stretch. It holds brown trout in the 1–1.5 kg range though there is always the chance of a larger fish. While there are stretches of good nymph water in the more stable sections, the river is generally more suited to spinning.

The lower reaches are often silt-laden from a tributary entering the west bank of the main river, so don't be discouraged by the appearance of the river at the main roadbridge on S.H.6 on the outskirts of Murchison. Floods in recent seasons have depleted the fish stocks.

Some years ago while on a deerstalking trip to the headwaters, I landed a superb brown trout weighing 5.6 kg on a Willesden Green spinner, from a pool above Downies Hut.

The Glenroy tributary, reached from the Glenroy Valley road, holds fish with an occasional trophy in the headwaters, if one is prepared to tramp beyond the road end and camp out. The lower reaches become easily silt-laden in a fresh.

Maruia River

Location and access   Rises in the Spenser Mountains and flows in a southerly direction through Cannibal Gorge to meet S.H.7 at Maruia Springs in the Lewis Pass. Follows S.H.7 to Springs Junction then turns north-west and follows S.H.65 and Shenandoah Road to join the Buller River 10 km south-west of Murchison. Access is not difficult from S.H.65 and from a number of side roads.

This moderate-sized river is highly recommended and holds good stocks of medium to large fish in clear mountain water flowing over a shingle and rock bed. (Drift figures reveal 100 fish/km at Paenga.) Above the Maruia Falls, the banks are lined with beech bush and clumps of manuka, while the lower reaches flow through willows. Below the Maruia Falls, formed during the Murchison earthquake, there are only brown trout, while above the falls there are both rainbow and brown.

There are only a few fish in the braided, unstable water above the Woolley confluence, but some are large. An old angling friend landed a 4.6 kg brown in this rough stretch on a minnow home-made from a chrysalis found on a macrocarpa. The best water is in the gorge west of Mt Rutland where the river leaves the road between Ruffe Creek and the Warwick Stream confluence. However, it takes a long day's tramp to negotiate the entire gorge.

For less energetic anglers there is excellent water upstream from West Bank bridge, at Peasoup Creek, Creighton Road and at Boundary Creek. Fish can be spotted and stalked with a dry fly or nymph in the smaller sizes, but a careful approach and a long leader is essential for success. The river takes some time to clear after heavy rain. There's also excellent spinning water in a number of spots, especially where fly casting is impossible.

Two small spawning tributaries crossing farmland, the Warwick and Rappahannock streams, hold fish. These lie between Burnbrae and Warwick Junction and are best fished early and late in the season in the lower reaches.

Woolley River

> **Location and access**   A small stream rising in the bush-covered Victoria Range flowing in a northerly direction and joining the Maruia near Maruia. Two kilometres south of Maruia the West Bank road crosses the Maruia and Woolley rivers.

The Woolley is a delightful clear stream offering spotting- and stalking-type dry fly and nymph fishing for browns and rainbows. The upper reaches flow through beech bush while the lower reaches meander across farmland. This stream is best fished either early or late in the season. Fish stocks are unreliable, but it tends to remain fishable when the Maruia is discoloured.

Lake Daniells

Location and access   Look for the sign on S.H.7 a few kilometres east of Springs Junction. An easy two-and-a-half-hour tramp through native bush on a well-defined track is required and the Manson–Nicholls Memorial Hut with 40 bunks is available for unsophisticated accommodation.

Season   Open all year except October.

This lake contains only rainbow but is surrounded by native bush and is worth visiting for the scenery alone. The shoreline can be waded in places, but generally the lake is best fished with a spinner.

West Coast District

This district stretches from the Heaphy River in the north to the Cascade River in the south. Geographically, this area comprises a long, narrow strip of coastal land west of the Southern Alps. For convenience the North-west Nelson Forest Park is described in this section, although rivers rising in the Park and draining into Nelson and Golden Bay are covered in the Nelson–Marlborough District.

The headwaters of most rivers lie in rugged, steep, bush- and snow-covered mountains and many of the rivers south of Harihari are snow and glacier fed. These rivers have a short, steep course to the sea, and with an annual rainfall between 2 000 mm on the Coast and up to 6 400 mm inland flash floods are common. Though some are silt-laden in summer when the snow melts, and provide a poor habitat for trout, there are a large number of excellent rain-fed bush rivers and spring-fed streams with stable beds that remain clear after rain or at least recover rapidly within a day or two.

Many of the rivers are rock- and stone-type waterways with dense bush covering the banks of the upper reaches. As a result some are inaccessible in these reaches, but trampers, mountaineers and deerstalkers often report sighting large brown trout in deep gorge pools where flooding does not unduly disturb fish stocks. The lower reaches of many of the rivers are swampy and difficult to reach without a boat. Despite high rainfall and flash floods there are some excellent lakes and rivers to fish on the Coast, and one could spend a lifetime exploring and fishing without covering all the water.

Those who have spent time exploring West Coast waters maintain this region offers the best fly fishing for brown trout in New Zealand. The scenery is superb, but take insect repellent and nylon overtrousers for protection against the sandflies and mosquitoes. As spring tends to be very wet, with a succession of westerly winds, the best period of the year to fish this region is from mid-January through to the end of March.

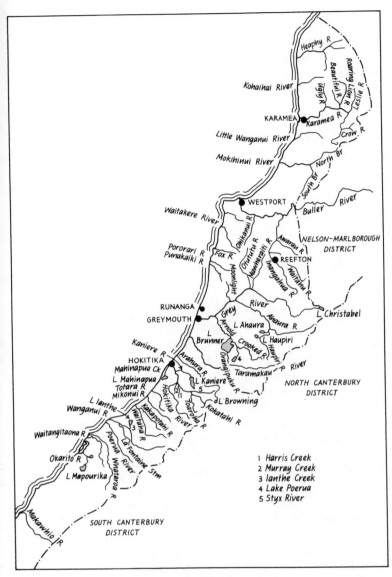

West Coast District (northern and middle section)

Rainbow trout are only present in the Taramakau, Arahura and Hokitika river systems and Lakes Brunner and Poerua. The other waters hold browns. Sockeye salmon have been liberated in Lake Poerua, but very few have been caught. Quinnat salmon run up the

Hokitika River in February–March, a few straying into the Taramakau, Arahura, Poerua, Cascade and even the Hollyford in South Westland.

Lake Mapourika holds resident quinnat salmon, and sea-run quinnat salmon enter the lake from the Okarito River, also in February–March. Similarly, salmon enter Lake Paringa from the Paringa and Hall rivers and spawn in the Windbag Stream. They also enter Lake Moeraki to spawn in the Moeraki (Blue) River. Nearly all the rivers and reasonable-sized creeks at some stage hold fish, many estuarine living or sea-run, but only the most productive waterways will be discussed.

Unless otherwise stated, the season opens on 1 October and closes on 30 April. Generally, the bag limit is 7 trout or salmon, except from Murray, Harris and Duck creeks, where the limit is 2 fish. Only 1 rainbow may be taken from the Arnold River catchment, including Lake Brunner, Lake Poerua, Orangipuku and Crooked rivers.

North-west Nelson Forest Park

This extensive block of remote, undeveloped country lies in the north-west corner of the South Island. It is the largest Forest Park in New Zealand, covering 405 786 ha, and contains some of the oldest and most complex rock formations on the West Coast. The country rises from near sea level to peaks over 1 700 m and is prone to the vagaries of north-west storms. Snow covers the tops in winter. Generally, the land is heavily bush-clad with few cut tramping tracks. Land formations have also been affected by the Murchison (1929) and Inangahua (1968) earthquakes. These have contributed to the ruggedness of the country, creating a number of small lakes from landslides. Several large rivers rise from these mountain ranges: in the north are the Heaphy, Aorere and Cobb; in the centre the Karamea and its many tributaries; in the south drain the Little Wanganui, Mokihinui, Matiri and Wangapeka. The Aorere, Cobb, Matiri and Wangapeka are described in the Nelson–Marlborough section.

It is strongly recommended that all who venture into the Park carry detailed maps and have an understanding of survival and tramping skills. Most rivers contain brown trout, but only those considered worth visiting are described. Within the confines of the Park lies the Tasman Wilderness Area in which helicopter access is prohibited. This area includes the headwaters of the Aorere River, the Roaring Lion, Beautiful and Ugly rivers, and the Karamea River from the Roaring Lion–Karamea junction to below the Ugly–Karamea junction. Helicopters are permitted to land at the Roaring Lion and Greys huts.

Unless otherwise specified, the season opens on 1 October and closes on 30 April, the bag limit is 4 trout, and the minimum length is 30 cm.

The Kohaihai River at the road end north of Karamea is a tea-stained stream holding a few brown trout but is probably only of interest to trampers walking the Heaphy Track.

Karamea River

Location   This is by far the largest river in the Park. The main river rises in the Allen Range where it saddles with the Little Wanganui and Wangapeka rivers. In the first part of its course the river flows north, but at the Leslie Junction (Big Bend) it turns to flow west, eventually reaching the Tasman Sea at Karamea township.

Access
From Karamea   the lower reaches can be fished. From here an arduous two-day tramp upriver takes you to the mouth of the Ugly tributary. The first hut upstream from Karamea is the 6-bunk Greys Hut, reached after a 4- to 5-hour tramp, the last three hours untracked.

From the Leslie Valley
- By tramping in over the Baton Saddle.
- From the Graham Valley near Ngatimoti, a two-day tramp over the Mt Arthur tableland.
- From the Trilobite Hut in the Cobb Valley via Lake Peel and Balloon Hut on the Mt Arthur tableland.

From the Wangapeka Track to Luna Hut at the headwaters of the Karamea. These last two routes are tracked, but tramping experience is advised.

From Nelson or Karamea by helicopter.

Season   Downstream from the mouth of the lower gorge it is open season all year round. Elsewhere, 1 October–30 April.

The Karamea River and tributaries offer wilderness brown trout fishing equal to the best in New Zealand. The main river from Luna Hut all the way to Karamea supplies an endless stock of self-sustaining fish averaging around 2 kg.

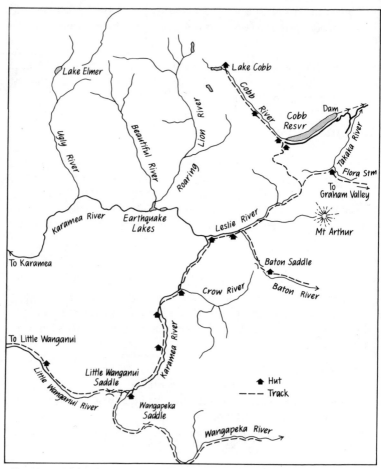

Karamea River System

The upper reaches above the Leslie confluence flow fast over a rock and stone bed and offer great nymph, dry and wet fly fishing to the agile boots-and-shorts angler (40 large fish/km have been counted on drift dives above Crow Hut). Fish can be spotted and stalked. The river is quite large by the time it reaches the Leslie Junction, but fish can still be spotted and the river forded with care (50 large fish/km at the Bend).

Near the Roaring Lion confluence lie the Earthquake Lakes formed during the Murchison earthquake, and these are well stocked with eels as well as trout. Spinning methods will take fish in all stretches but especially in the Earthquake Lakes. Below the Roaring Lion the country becomes very remote and the river gorgy, so angling pressure is minimal, yet there is still superb water.

At Karamea the river is very large, slower flowing and more suited to spinning, but there's an evening rise when conditions are favourable and trout can be taken on a fly. Drift dives at Arapito reveal good stocks of mainly medium-sized trout (100 fish/km).

Karamea tributaries

All reasonable-sized tributaries contain fish, but only five will be described.

Crow

The Crow Hut at the Karamea–Crow junction offers 'back-country accommodation' and a base for fishing this highly regarded stream. The river flows in a westerly direction. The fish population is high, but not all are in good condition and poor fish should be returned. The stream is easily waded and best fished in boots and longs for sandfly protection.

This is a typical clear bush stream with a rock and stone riverbed and fish can readily be stalked providing you keep out of sight. Fish are not sophisticated feeders and will take a wide range of carefully presented dry flies and nymphs. Try Mole Fly, Coch-y-bondhu, Royal Wulff and Palmer dry flies or Half Back, Hare and Copper, Perla and Pheasant Tail nymphs in sizes 10–16.

Leslie

This is the most accessible tributary, and the Leslie Hut or the Karamea Bend Hut on the Karamea offer the best base. It flows south from the Mt Arthur tableland to enter the Karamea River at the Big Bend. I first fished this stream in 1962 when the trout were prolific. A size 12 home-tied weighted Red Tipped Governor nymph proved deadly and I spent time hooking fish and handing the rod to my three deerstalking companions and watching their novice antics. For a few years the fishing fell away, but recently the trout have come back. Flies and conditions as for the Crow.

Roaring Lion

Access
- A hard day's tramp down the Karamea from Big Bend.
- From the Cobb Valley either via Kimbell Spur or from Chaffey Hut via Chaffey Stream and Breakfast Creek.
- From the Ugly or Aorere headwaters via Aorere Saddle. Experienced trampers only should tackle these routes.
- Via helicopter to the Roaring Lion Hut.

This is a marvellous river offering similar conditions to the Crow and the Leslie, but it is larger and fords are tricky in the lower reaches, some more than waist deep. The river flows in a southerly direction through heavily forested, rugged country. Good fishing is available upstream as far as Breakfast Creek. There are trophy fish in this river. In 1984, using a Red Palmer dry fly, I landed a brown in superb condition weighing a shade under 4 kg. Use the same flies as for the Crow. There's a good evening rise, but the sandflies are fierce. Catch and release is strongly recommended.

Beautiful River
This tributary can be easily reached across from the Roaring Lion Hut providing the Roaring Lion is fordable. Only the lower 1–2 km is worth fishing, beyond which the river rises steeply and becomes very rough going. There are a few good pools in the first kilometre and trout are easy to spot.

Ugly River

Access   This is the most remote tributary and only experienced trampers should attempt to reach this valley – either upstream from Karamea, downstream from the Roaring Lion or via the Roaring Lion headwaters.

There is excellent water between McNabb and Domett creeks as well as in the lower reaches where the river is deep and swift. The river flows in a southerly direction from Lake Elmer, formed by a landslide in the Murchison earthquake. The lake itself holds fish, but in my experience they are in poor condition and not worth taking unless you are short of food. Fishing methods and conditions for the Ugly are similar to those for the other tributaries described. The river holds less water than the Roaring Lion, but it contains the odd trophy fish and clears rapidly after a fresh. Two friends and I destroyed a gill net at a campsite on this river. On the same trip, we ate venison, trout and eel.

Rafters have negotiated the Karamea River, but the gorge below Kakapo River is rather terrifying. The Kakapo itself is well worth exploring.

Little Wanganui River

Location and access   Drains the Scarlett and Allen ranges south of the Karamea River system, flows on a westerly course and enters the Tasman Sea at Little Wanganui some 15 km south of Karamea township. The lower reaches can be reached off S.H.67. A side road follows the river upstream on the true right bank to the start of the Wangapeka Track to Nelson. The Little Wanganui Hut, which sleeps 18 persons, is some 2–3 hours' tramp upstream and this provides a reasonable base for fishing.

Season   Open all year downstream from the Ministry of Works riverflow-gauging cableway. Elsewhere, 1 October–30 April.

There are sea-run trout in the lower reaches, especially when whitebait are running early in the season. The lower reaches are rather unstable and shingly, but the upper reaches offer more stable water in virgin native bush to the tramper/angler who can cast accurately to easily spotted trout.

Mokihinui River

Location   This river drains a very large catchment of rugged bush country including the Radiant, Allen, Matiri and Lyell ranges. The north and south branches, respectively, flow north and south to The Forks. The main river then flows in a westerly direction to enter the sea at Mokihinui, some 40 km north of Westport.

Access
- From Mokihinui by tramping upstream on a rough track following the south bank of the river. The Forks Hut is a good 6 hours' tramp from the road end. Sinclair Hut is only 30 minutes' walk across the river flats from Forks Hut. Goat Creek Hut is another 3 hours' tramp up the south branch.

- By tramping over Kiwi Saddle into the Johnson tributary from the Wangapeka Track.
- By helicopter. The fixed-wing airstrip at The Forks is at present unserviceable.

Season   Open all year below the Ministry of Works riverflow gauge. Elsewhere, 1 October–30 April.

This is a superb remote brown trout fishery almost rivalling its northern neighbour, the Karamea, though considerably smaller. There are extensive stretches of clear mountain water with fish averaging 2 kg (30 large fish/km in the north and south branches). This rock-and stone-type back-country river winds through dense beech forest and across tussock flats. Trout can be spotted and stalked and respond to a wide selection of dry flies and nymphs.

All major tributaries hold fish, the Johnson, Allen, Hemphill, Larrikin and Hennessy creeks being especially recommended. The lower reaches offer sea-run fish to spinners or a smelt fly when the whitebait are running, especially after a fresh.

Buller River (below Lyell) and tributaries

Buller River
(See Nelson–Marlborough District for the Upper Buller.)

Location and access   From Murchison, the river passes through the Upper Buller Gorge, flows more sedately through Inangahua then enters the Lower Buller Gorge before discharging into the Tasman Sea at Westport. S.H.6 from Murchison to Westport follows the river.

Season   Open season all year round on the Buller below Lyell.

While the upper reaches above Murchison are manageable and can be fished with a fly, this section below Lyell is heavy, deep water and best fished with a spinner or live bait. Good fish are taken near the mouth on a silver spinner early in the season when whitebait are running. Fish tend to be smaller in this section of river compared with the upper reaches.

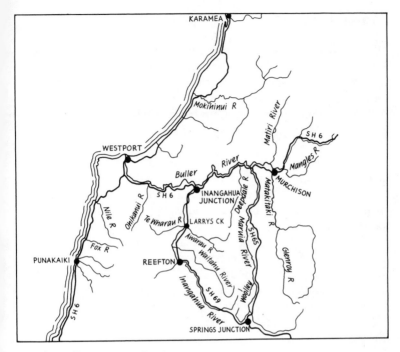

Lower Buller River and tributaries

Inangahua River

> **Location and access**   Rises in the Rahu Saddle area and flows north
> through Reefton to enter the Buller at Inangahua. S.H.7 follows
> the upper reaches to Reefton while S.H.69 continues to Inangahua.

This large tributary is over 60 km in length and contains brownish,
peat-stained water over a rock and stone bed. The river is lined by
bush, willows and scrub. Fish can be spotted in ideal conditions and
taken on dry flies and nymphs, but the river holds sufficient trout
for 'blind' fishing methods to be successful. In the past, open-cast
coalmining operations have polluted the river below Garvey Creek,
but in spite of this good stocks of trout have been seen on drift dives,
especially in the vicinity of Inangahua Landing (30 large fish/km).
Upstream from Reefton fish tend to be smaller although stocks are
still good, especially in the vicinity of Blacks Point and Crushington
where there are some deep holes.

Waitahu River

Location and access This major tributary of the Inangahua River drains the Victoria Range and flows on a north-westerly course to enter the Inangahua 5 km north-west of Reefton. Cammons Road from S.H.69 leads to and crosses the river. From here a four-wheel-drive and walking track leads upstream on the true right bank as far as the Montgomerie River confluence.

This is a pleasant peat-stained scenic river holding good-sized browns in clear pools and runs to well beyond the confluence of the Waitahu and Montgomerie rivers. They present quite a challenge during low water flows in summer but a cautious approach and fine gear should bring results.

The river has been polluted by coal fines from time to time and is quite heavily fished and poached by the locals. Try Coch-y-bondhu, Red Tipped Governor, Royal Wulff and Twilight Beauty dry flies or Hare and Copper, Caddis, Half Back and Pheasant Tail nymphs, all in sizes 14–18. Use a long trace and be careful not to line the fish. There is 10 km of good water and the nor'wester tends to blow up the valley.

Te Wharau River

Location and access Drains the bush-covered ranges north-west of Reefton, flows east and enters the Inangahua River just upstream from Larry's Creek. A side road leaves S.H.69 between Larry's Creek and Rotokohu, follows Fletcher Creek upstream to coalmines, and leads to the middle reaches of the Te Wharau. The lower reaches can be fished by crossing on a swingbridge over the Inangahua River.

Te Wharau is a typical boots-and-shorts West Coast river with a boulder and shingle bed and well-defined pools. Fish are easily spotted in clear water, but the river rises rapidly in a fresh.

Larry's Creek (Awarau)

Location and access Flows through bush country on a parallel course north of the Waitahu and joins the Inangahua 12 km north-west of Reefton on S.H.69. Access to this river is on foot from the end of the forestry road up the true right bank.

Another boots-and-shorts stream, the Awarau is similar to but smaller than the Waitahu. It has a reputation for the occasional large fish, especially early in the season, and fish up to 4.5 kg have been taken. However, these fish have grown to this size for a very good reason – they are wily and cunning! Use the same methods as for the Waitahu.

Ohikanui River

Location and access   This river flows on a northerly course to join the Buller 15 km east of Westport. S.H.6 crosses the river near its mouth.

This is a clear, swift, rough, bouldery, boots-and-shorts river flowing through virgin bush country. Clear pools and runs offer excellent sport to the angler prepared to tramp and camp upriver. Fish stocks are high away from the road end. There are no huts in this valley. Wear nylon overtrousers for the sandflies and take insect repellent.

The really adventurous angler should try the Deepdale River joining the Buller River higher up near Newton Flat. The Buller needs to be crossed by boat unless you tramp in from S.H.65 at Glengarry.

The Haupiri River offers good fishing in well-defined pools and runs.

Between Westport and Greymouth S.H.6 crosses a number of small rivers holding brown trout. Although these rain-fed streams are not highly recommended they are worth exploring by tramper/anglers visiting the Paparoa National Park. Sea-run trout can also be caught in the estuaries when the whitebait are running early in the season. These include the Nile or Waitakere river at Charleston, the Fox River at Tiromoana, the Pororari and Punakaiki rivers at Punakaiki and Ten Mile Creek just south of Greigs. The Pororari is the most interesting of these rivers.

Grey River and tributaries

Grey River

Location   This large river system drains the country from the Main Divide to the coast and from Reefton in the north to Lake Brunner in the south. The main river tends to follow a south-westerly course and discharges into the Tasman Sea at Greymouth.

Access
Upper reaches
- From Palmer Road, which is not signposted and is easily missed. The road leaves S.H.7 4 km from Springs Junction on a sharp bend and runs south almost to the Robinson River confluence. This is a very scenic, bush-lined road which eventually emerges into cleared farmland. The Brown Grey is the first tributary on your right, followed by the Blue Grey draining Lake Christabel on your left at the first farm. Both are worth fishing, as is the Robinson River at the road end.
- From Hukarere (the Snowy River turn-off) just north of Ikamatua on S.H.7 to Hukawai, McVicars and the Alexander River confluence.
- From Waipuna Road off S.H.7 6 km north of Totara Flat. This road also leads to the Clarke River.

Lower and middle reaches   S.H.7 follows the true left bank from Ikamatua to Greymouth

Season   Open season all year round below the Clarke confluence. Elsewhere, 1 October–30 April.

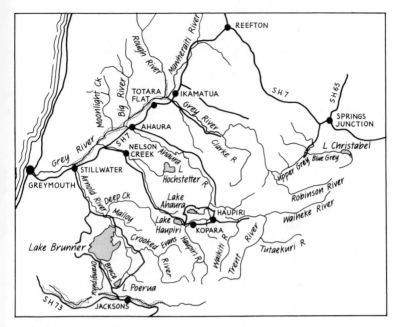

Grey River System

This is a very large river which, as it drains an enormous catchment, is very prone to flooding, especially in the lower reaches. It may take four or five days to clear after heavy rain. However, at Waipuna there are excellent stocks of mainly medium-sized fish in quite heavy water (240 fish/km). Further upstream, there is superb fly fishing in clear rock- and stone-type water, and the fish tend to be larger. The banks vary between farmland, tussock, scrub and beech bush, and fish can be spotted but are shy. Vegetation lining the banks produces an abundance of cicadas and beetles, there is a good mayfly hatch and caddis are plentiful under stones.

Don't expect to take a limit, but the Upper Grey offers quality West Coast fishing. There is approximately 15 km of unroaded river through the Gentle Annie Gorge between the end of the road from Hukawai and McVicars to the end of Palmer Road running south from Springs Junction. This is great back-country fishing for the energetic angler. Try Mole Fly, Royal Wulff, and deer-hair pattern dry flies, weighted nymphs or Orange Rabbit and Parson's Glory lures. The lower and middle reaches, where the water is wide and deep, are best fished with spinning gear. Many anglers use live bait.

The Robinson, Brown and Blue Grey tributaries (catch and release is recommended in the latter two) have already been mentioned. Most reasonable-sized tributaries hold fish, but there are far too many to detail, so only the larger ones are described here.

Clarke River

This river joins the Grey upstream from Waipuna and access, as for the Upper Grey, is off Waipuna Road. Fish average 1–2 kg and there is good, clear fly water.

Mawheraiti River (Little Grey)

> **Location and access**   Rises near Reefton and follows S.H.7 to Ikamatua where it joins the Grey. Take the metalled road which leaves S.H.7 opposite the Mawheraiti Hotel, south from Mawheraiti township. This leads to good water on the true right bank. There is a long walk across the railway line and farmland from S.H.7 further downstream.

A typical tea-coloured stream, the Mawheraiti holds good stocks of fish averaging 0.75–1.25 kg. Fish are hard to spot, but try the runs with a well-weighted Hare and Copper nymph. There are few fish above Mawheraiti after the last major flood, though it recovers rapidly after a fresh.

Rough River (Otututu)

> **Location and access**   Rises on the eastern side of the Paparoa Range and flows for 30 km on a south-easterly course to join the Grey at Ikamatua. Access to the lower reaches from Ikamatua on Atarau Road. Anglers need to tramp the river to reach the best fishing. This valley has no tracks or huts.

The Rough is a very popular, boisterous, bouldery, rock-and-stone river flowing through native bush and holding fish up to 4.5 kg. Trout can be spotted in clear water, but many will be missed in the rough white water, and they must be approached with caution and skill. It's a boots-and-shorts stream for the adventurous and fit, with over 15 km of fishable water to well above the Gordon Creek confluence, the best fishing being upstream from Mirfin Creek.

Early morning reflections on Lake Poerua.

Guides bring paying clients to this river and many fly in by helicopter. A friend did just that a couple of years ago but encountered torrential rain for four days and was glad to be flown out without wetting his line in the river. Such is fishing on the West Coast! Catch and release recommended.

The Big River at Slaty Creek and the Moonlight Creek at Atarau both hold fish. These are small, clear, shingle and bouldery streams draining bush country. Access is off Atarau and Moonlight Valley roads.

Ahaura River

Location and access   Saddles with the Doubtful and Hope rivers of the Lake Sumner Forest Park and flows on a westerly course to enter the Grey at Ahaura. Drains Lakes Ahaura and Haupiri. This is a large river, especially in the middle and lower reaches. The lower reaches are gorgy and rather inaccessible. The middle reaches can be reached off the Ahaura–Kopara road (Watterson Road), the upper reaches from the Kopara–Haupiri road or the Haupiri–Amuri road via Nelson Creek.

This clear, swiftly flowing river joins the Grey 30 km above Greymouth. The fly angler should head for the upper reaches where there is excellent water holding good-sized fish, especially well above the Haupiri confluence. The river is still quite large and shingly in this area, but fish stocks are good and fish can be spotted in bright low water conditions (33 large fish/km). Above the Haupiri confluence the water is clear, but below the Haupiri the water becomes tea-coloured.

Access to the Waikiti, Waiheke, Tutaekuri and Trent rivers can be achieved by tramping from the end of the Haupiri–Amuri road at Haupiri. These are all excellent, remote, back-country, boots-and-shorts rivers offering quality fishing and the chance of a trophy fish. The Waikiti Valley is rough going. For the tramper/angler, the Trent is most favoured. Here you are unlikely to be disturbed by other anglers, though the sandflies are big enough to shoot! Trout are easily spotted in clear water.

Haupiri River

Location and access   There are two branches to this river. The clear-water rain- and snow-fed branch rises close to Harper Pass, then follows a north-westerly direction flowing through bush-clad mountains before joining the other heavily peat-stained branch draining Lake Haupiri. Gradually the clear and brown waters mingle in the main river, which enters the Ahaura at Haupiri. Take the Nelson Creek–Kopara road to Haupiri School. The private Wallace Road follows the clear tributary upstream. Permission is required. The main river is crossed just before the school and access is not difficult.

Across the farmland, the clear-water tributary has been modified by stopbanks although there are still some good brown trout in well-defined pools and runs. Upstream from the farm there is excellent water for fly fishing with easily spotted fish up to 4 kg in large pools as far up as the hot springs (8 km above the farm). This is boots-and-shorts fishing with plenty of walking required in a back-country rock and stone river. The present landowner is a conservationist and encourages fly fishing and catch and release in this section of river.

The confluence of these tributaries lies just upstream from the roadbridge and can be reached from an obscure bush track 0.5 km upstream from the bridge. Fish stocks are very high in this section of water (200 fish/km). Trout can be seen lying along the line where the clear and brown lake waters mingle.

A small side creek, Clear Stream, enters just above this confluence and always holds a few fish in gin-clear, still water. These present a real challenge. Downstream from the roadbridge the river becomes quite large, flowing over a shingle bed and across farmland, but it holds a good stock of browns in the 1–2 kg range. These can be caught on flies and spinners.

Arnold River

Location Drains Lake Brunner at Moana and flows in a northerly direction to enter the Grey River at Stillwater on S.H.7 about 10 km from Greymouth. There is a hydro-electric dam 13 km below Lake Brunner at Kaimata and the water which backs up for 4 km is known as Lake Ullstrom.

Access From Arnold Road to Lake Brunner at Stillwater, Kokiri, Aratika, Kotuku and the lake outlet. There's good water off Blairs Block Road to Kohatu. Turn off and cross the river at the meat processing works.

Season Open all year between Lake Brunner and the Arnold Dam. Elsewhere, 1 October–30 April.

Restrictions The bag limit for rainbow trout only, in the Arnold and tributaries, is 1 fish.

This large, fast-flowing, medium-sized, tea-stained tributary of the Grey, holding very large numbers of brown and the occasional rainbow trout averaging 1–2 kg, is highly regarded and heavily fished although access is rather limited. The banks are covered in places by native bush and in other stretches by willows. Steve Barclay told me it used to be called 'Duffer's Creek' by local Greymouth anglers as anyone could catch a fish. Most fishing is done on the lower 11 km below the dam, but drift dives have also revealed high numbers of fish above the dam at Kotuku (240 fish/km at Kotuku, 75 fish/km at Kokiri).

The river is stable and seldom floods but can become discoloured for two or three days after heavy rain from silt-laden water entering from Malloy and Deep creeks. It is very difficult to fish when Lake Brunner is high. Fish, which often lie deep, cannot be spotted, and the stones are slippery to wade over. The insect life is prolific. Try a well-weighted nymph on a sink-tipped line and a long trace, a small wet March Brown or Twilight Beauty on a sinking line, or a well-hackled dry fly such as Mole Fly, Coch-y-bondhu or a deer-hair pattern. At times, a green beetle imitation can be deadly. In the evening, fish will rise to a Twilight Beauty. Fish can also be taken on a spinner or a night lure such as Mrs Simpson and Hairy Dog fished on a sinking line.

Two small tea-coloured streams, Deep Creek and the Malloy Creek, join the Arnold at Kotuku, north of Moana. Both hold fish and are well worth investigating, especially in low water conditions. Deep Creek often has a thin oil slick on the surface where a natural seepage has been occurring for many years. The Arnold Valley road crosses both creeks near Kotuku Rail Station.

The Grey Valley lakes and adjacent rivers

Of a number of lakes in the Grey catchment only four can be recommended for fishing. The water in all these lakes is a tea colour, making fish spotting virtually impossible. Blind fishing with spinners or flies or trolling from boats are the recommended techniques, though live-bait fishing is also practised.

Lake Brunner

Season   Open season all year round in this lake apart from within 30 m of any stream mouth.

Restrictions   The bag limit, for rainbow trout only, in this lake and the streams entering or leaving it is 1 fish. Seven brown trout may be taken.

At 10 km across this is the largest lake in the area. Most of the shoreline is covered in native bush. Deep trolling accounts for most fish although the outlet is a hot spot for live bait fishing after dark. For trollers, the Crooked Delta (Howitt Point), Hohonu Delta (Hohonu Spit), and the Orangapuku Delta (Swan Bay) are good areas, especially late in the season when fish are gathering for their spawning runs. Varieties of Toby and Cobra spinners take most fish.

In low-water conditions, the mouth of the Orangapuku River is well worth a visit by shore fly anglers, especially towards evening. There is a marked track off the road to Mitchells. Try blind lure fishing with a medium-sinking line and a dark fly such as Hairy Dog, Mrs Simpson or Fuzzy Wuzzy. When the lake is high, this area is difficult to reach. Fly casting from a boat is good in the lower reaches of the Orangapuku and Bruce rivers where the trout population is very high.

Orangapuku River

Location and access This stream flows almost from the Taramakau River valley round the base of the Hohonu Range and joins Bruce Creek just before entering Swan Bay at the southern end of Lake Brunner. The Mitchells–Inchbonnie road crosses the lower reaches of the Orangapuku.

Only the lower 3 km of the Orangapuku is worth fishing, as water flows above this level can be unreliable. This is a clear-water stream where fish can be easily spotted. The river is shingly and rapidly becomes unfishable after heavy rain. The banks are lined by patches of willow, native bush and gorse. Stocks are not high and fishing is best late in the season when a spawning run of browns occurs.

Bruce Creek

Location and access Drains swampy land near the southern end of Lake Poerua, skirts the base of Mt Te Kinga and joins the Orangapuka upstream from Swan Bay. Take the northernmost side road off the Mitchells–Inchbonnie road. This runs towards Mt Te Kinga and crosses the stream at an old farm bridge. It pays to seek permission from the landowner, but this is seldom refused.

The Bruce is an entirely different stream from the Orangapuku, being spring fed and remaining clear after rain. There are some deep holes and fast-flowing runs, but generally the stream flows placidly across farmland. The water is a weak tea colour, the stone riverbed brownish and weedy. Fish can sometimes be spotted. Stocks of brown trout are deceptively high, as fish often remain hidden during the day under long strands of green weed. There is sometimes an evening rise on warm summer evenings. Trout then appear in great numbers and feed voraciously. Fish, which average 1.3 kg with an occasional one up to 2.5 kg, can be taken by skilful fly anglers, but catch and release is recommended. About 1 km upstream from the farm bridge the stream divides into three. The middle tributary offers a further 1 km of challenging water where fish can be more easily spotted on patches of sandy riverbed. Use small dry flies and weighted nymphs on a long trace. During the evening rise try a sparsely hackled Twilight Beauty wet fly fished upstream. This spot is strongly recommended to the purist.

Crooked River

Location and access   Drains the Alexander Range and flows in a north-easterly direction to enter the eastern side of Lake Brunner south of Howitt Point. It's 11 km by road south from Moana to Te Kinga where the river is first reached. Take the road from Te Kinga to Rotomanu. The Bell Hill–Inchbonnie road crosses higher upstream at the Crooked River Reserve. A rough private farm road follows upstream on the true left bank to the confluence of the Evans River tributary and then follows this river for a further 6 km. Permission must be obtained from the landowner.

Quite a large river in the lower reaches, which are best fished from a boat, there is excellent clear fly water across private farmland in the vicinity of Rotomanu and upstream as far as the Bell Hill–Inchbonnie roadbridge. The river gorges above this bridge. Upstream from the gorge, there is a limited amount of fishing water to just above the Evans River junction and the farm bridge. Fish can sometimes be spotted in the pocket water along the edges of pools, but do not neglect fishing some of the fast water blind with a good floating dry fly or a heavily weighted nymph.

The Crooked River above the Evans River confluence is worth exploring for the boots-and-shorts angler, but again the river gorges. There are some good fish in these difficult, deep holes overhung by native bush. The Evans River is a major spawning stream for Lake Brunner but is unstable, fast flowing and has no holding water so is not worth fishing.

The Eastern Hohonu River entering Lake Brunner just north of Bain Bay on the western shore also holds fish but is generally more suited to spinning. The lower reaches are slow flowing and log jammed. There are stretches off the forestry roads from Kaimata which are worth exploring by the angler not afraid to tramp. The mouth should be fished from a boat.

Lake Poerua

Season   1 November to 30 April.

Restrictions   The bag limit for rainbow is 1 fish. Total limit, 7 trout.

Boat-launching facilities   At Te Kinga Reserve.

This lake holds both rainbow and browns which have very orange flesh from eating koura (freshwater crayfish). Sockeye salmon were released here in 1984. Most fish are caught by trolling. There is some shoreline fly fishing along the eastern and swampy southern shore in November–December before the shallow lake becomes weedy. Casting a large Greenwell's Glory or Royal Wulff dry fly from a drifting boat along the bush-covered western shore can bring results.

Poerua River

Location and access   Drains the northern end of Lake Poerua, then skirts the bush-clad Mt Te Kinga, and flows in a northerly direction for 7 km before joining the Crooked River in the vicinity of Lake Whitestone. Take Station Road off the Inchbonnie–Rotomanu road to Rotomanu Rail Station and then Hodgkinson Road. The river parallels the railway line on its western side.

This willow-lined, tea-coloured stream flowing across farmland is lined by native bush on its true left bank. It holds a moderate stock of browns averaging 1–1.3 kg, but fish are not easy to spot and the shingle riverbed is slippery to cross.

Lake Haupiri

Access   From the Nelson Creek–Kopara road.

Boat-launching facilities   On the bush-lined shore off this road.

This attractive wildlife reserve surrounded by bush and farmland is best fished from a boat. The lake water is heavily peat-stained.

Lake Hochstetter

Access From a signposted side road off the Nelson Creek–Kopara road. Boats can be launched on this lake.

Most fish are caught by trolling. The lake is attractively bush-lined though some fly fishing is possible from the shore in low water conditions.

There's good dry fly water at Clear Stream.

Taramakau River

Location   Saddles with the Hurunui River at Harper Pass, flows on a westerly course to meet S.H.73 and the Otira River at Aickens and eventually reaches the sea near Kumara Junction.

Access   From S.H.73 which follows the river and then the tramping track upstream in the direction of Harper Pass. Taramakau is a large river and although it is rather unstable and shingly and prone to flooding, it does hold brown and rainbows along with a small run of quinnat salmon in February–March.

Season   Open all year only below the bridge at Jacksons.

The river has improved since dredging operations ceased in 1981 but can take four to five days to clear after rain. Drift dives have revealed good stocks of mainly brown trout as far downstream as Kumara (40 fish/km at Kumara). There are some good pools near Dillmanstown and reasonable water at Jacksons. Fish can be taken on dry and wet flies, nymphs and spinners. Local knowledge is useful in locating good stable water as the river can change after a flood.

The Taipo River enters the Taramakau 10 km west of Jacksons and is crossed by S.H.73 close to its confluence. It holds small numbers of brown trout but is even more unstable and flood prone than the Taramakau, but there's some attractive water upstream from the gorge.

Nicholas Stream and Clear Stream

Location and access   These small streams rise separately from the Hohonu Range and flow parallel to, but north of, the Taramakau River in the vicinity of the Taramakau settlement. They can be reached across private farmland from the end of Nicholas Road. Nicholas Stream flows closer to the Taramakau River in old river channels of the main river. Some writers have stated that Nicholas Stream is sometimes known as Clear Stream. This is incorrect.

These clear, spring-fed streams hold good-sized browns among weed and willows which present quite a challenge in still-water fishing for the angler adept at stalking trout. Only the lower 2 km of Clear Stream is worth fishing although there is an occasional fish further upstream. The fishing can be very rewarding for the skilful dry fly and nymph angler fishing with fine gear, a long trace and small flies. Keep low, avoid wading, dress in neutral colours, wear polaroids and cast accurately.

These streams seldom discolour after rain, but stock wading in the river and farm machinery fording can adversely affect the fishing. Fish rise well during the day but are selective feeders. Catch and release strongly recommended. Permission is required from the landowner.

Arahura River

> **Location and access** Rises east of Lake Kaniere and enters the sea 6 km north of Hokitika. Access off S.H.6 at the mouth, Arahura Valley Road, Humphreys Gully Road and from the Milltown road in the upper reaches via Lake Kaniere. The Milltown road crosses the river higher up.
>
> **Season** Open all year below Humphries Road at the lower gorge.

This is a moderately large river with well-defined pools and runs crossing farmland. Gold dredging ceased here in 1960, and the upper reaches have long been a source of greenstone. The Arahura has clear water in the upper reaches with a boulder and shingle bed and is easily waded during normal conditions but tends to flood easily, and having a large watershed it may take four to five days to clear. It contains brown trout with a few rainbow in the upper reaches. The energetic angler should tramp beyond the roadbridge from the Milltown road where there is excellent water upstream as far as Newton Creek. Some sea-run browns can be caught near the mouth either on a silvery spinner or a smelt fly during the whitebait season in September–November.

Hokitika River

> **Location and access** Rises in the Southern Alps and flows north-west to Hokitika where it enters the Tasman Sea. S.H.6 crosses near the mouth at Kaniere; there's good access at Kokatahi and from roads in the region of Kowhiterangi.
>
> **Season** Open all year downstream from the lower gorge. Elsewhere, 1 October–30 April.

The Hokitika is a large, unstable, flood-prone, shingly river, but below

S.H.6 it offers sea-run browns in the whitebait season and a reasonable run of quinnat salmon in February–March. These initially came from fry released by a commercial venture started on the Kaniere River in 1979. There are browns, especially in the lower reaches, and good-sized rainbows above the gorge in the upper reaches where conditions are more stable. For the fit angler it is well worth tramping into the headwaters and up the Whitcombe tributary in search of these rainbows.

Hokitika tributaries

Kaniere River

Location and access   Drains the northern end of Lake Kaniere and eventually joins the Hokitika River. Access off Lake Kaniere road.

The Kaniere holds browns with salmon entering the river in February–April. Since having been modified for hydro-electric power generation it has not been highly valued as a trout fishery. The upper

Casting into the scenic Styx River.

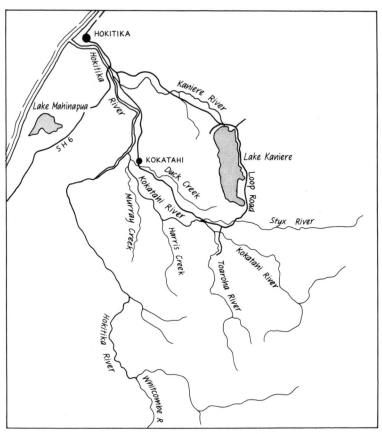

Hokitika River System

reaches are heavily bush-lined, but below the power station there is fishable water, though it's tea-coloured, fast flowing and best suited to spinning.

Kokatahi River

Location and access   Joins the Hokitika at Kokatahi. Access off Upper Kokatahi Road and Lake Kaniere Loop Road south of Kaniere Lodge.

Season   Open all year downstream from the Styx confluence.

This stream is similar to the parent river in being unstable and flood-prone, but upstream from the upper bridge there is much better, stable, bush-lined water where dry flies and nymphs will succeed. Fish can be spotted in clear, bright conditions and are mainly small to medium-sized browns. Stocks are not great, however.

Styx River

> **Location and access**   Flows just south of Lake Kaniere to join the Kokatahi a few kilometres below the upper bridge on the upper Kokatahi Road.

The Styx holds small browns and a few rainbow which can be seen and fished for in clear pools and runs. There is excellent water upstream from the upper bridge. Very scenic in the upper reaches with native bush covering the banks, but beware of the sandfly swarms. There is at least 8 km to explore beyond the road end.

Toaroha River

> **Access**   Very similar to the Styx, with access from a side road off the Upper Kokatahi Road just south of the Styx River.

The bush-clad upper reaches above the gorge are recommended to the tramper/angler. Clear rock and stone river where fish can be spotted.

Duck, Harris and Murray Creeks

> **Location and access**   Access to Duck Creek is from the Upper Kokatahi Road, to Harris Creek from Cropp and Ford roads and to Murray Creek also from Ford Road.
>
> **Restrictions**   The bag limit is 2 fish.

These small, stable, spring-fed streams flow over private farmland and join the Kokatahi River near Kokatahi. Duck Creek lies north of the main river while Harris and Murray creeks lie to the south. All three creeks hold browns up to 1 kg which are not easy to deceive in narrow, clear spring water. After a fresh, when other rivers are dirty, these creeks are well worth a visit. When hooked, fish make a dive for the weed beds. They can often be retrieved by allowing the line to go slack for a time. There is an evening rise in suitable conditions. Use very small dry flies and nymphs on long, fine tippets and keep out of sight. All these creeks suffer to some extent from dairy farming operations.

Lake Kaniere

This is a very attractive, bush-lined lake suitable only for trolling and water-skiing. It holds browns and perch in tea-coloured water. Though open all year except within 30 m of stream mouths, it is not greatly recommended to the angler.

Lake Mahinapua

Location and access   This scenic lake, which is open for fishing all year, lies between S.H.6 and the coast 10 km south of Hokitika.

Boat-launching facilities   At Shanghai Bay off Ruatapu Road on the western shore.

This lake is similar to Lake Kaniere in providing boat fishing for browns and perch.

Totara River

Location and access   S.H.6 crosses the river just north of Ross, while Totara Valley Road gives access to the upper reaches. A scramble down through bush and scrub is required to reach the river.

The Totara is a brown, bouldery, bush-stained stream with reasonable brown trout fishing only in the upper reaches. Lower down it tends to be unstable. Fish are not easy to spot and average 1 kg.

Mikonui River

Location and access   Enters the sea just south of Ross. S.H.6 crosses near the mouth. Totara Valley Road crosses the Totara Saddle and leads to the upper reaches at Gribben Flat. This is a long, narrow, rough, metalled road with two or three fords and is more suitable for four-wheel-drive vehicles.

The meandering Duck Creek flows through private farmland near Kokatahi.

The Mikonui is a medium-sized, clear, rock and stone river which is rather unstable and flood-prone but still holds a reasonable stock of good-sized brown trout. There are a few pools upstream from the main roadbridge if one is prepared to walk. The best water lies both upstream and downstream at the end of the road at Gribben Flat. This is private farmland and the present owners live in Ross, but permission to fish is readily granted. Upstream the south branch (Tuke River) ends in an impressive but unfishable gorge. The north branch (Mikonui) has a good spawning run late in the season. Try size 14–16 weighted nymphs on a long trace with care not to line spotted fish. A deer-hair dry fly is also most effective.

Ellis Creek

Location and access   This small, stable, tea-coloured tributary of the Waitaha River joins the main river just upstream on the north side of the main S.H.6 bridge. Waitaha Valley Road crosses higher upstream. The confluence of Ellis Creek and the Waitaha can be seen from S.H.6 bridge.

Ellis Creek is worth exploring with a fly late in the season for 1 km upstream. It holds small browns, but stocks are not high. The Ellis remains clear when the main river is silt-laden. The Waitaha rivers (Big and Little) are too unstable to be recommended, though they do hold the occasional fish.

Lake Ianthe

S.H.6 skirts the eastern shore of this small, shallow, scenic lake, but it's hardly worth fishing, though it does hold some brown trout. The best fishing is from a boat or with spinning gear, but weed can be a problem. This lake is open all year.

La Fontaine Stream

> **Location and access**   This tea-coloured, weedy, spring-fed stream drains a swamp south of Harihari and flows across farmland in a northerly direction to enter the Wanganui River north of that township. Access across private farmland from side roads off Wanganui Flat Road and La Fontaine Road.

Regarded by many anglers as the finest fly fishing river on the West Coast, La Fontaine is only 16 km long, but there is fishable water from as far downstream as one can get, to the main roadbridge upstream. The middle and lower reaches are lined with flax and patches of bush, but there is plenty of fishable water. The river is well stocked; fish average 0.75–1 kg and can sometimes be spotted, but are scary. During the day try Dad's Favourite and Kakahi Queen dry flies and Hare and Copper and Pheasant Tail nymphs, all in sizes 14–18. For the rise try Twilight Beauty in size 14 or March Brown and Twilight Beauty wet flies in sizes 10–14. It seems amazing that live-bait fishing is still permitted on this stream.

Waitangitaona River

> **Location and access**   This spring-fed river drains swampy country around Whataroa, skirts the northern boundary of the Okarito State Forest, and enters the sea just north of the Okarito Lagoon. Access through the village of Rotokino off the Whataroa Flat road on Purcell and Gunn roads and tracks across private farmland.

In about 1965 a major flood altered the course of this river and directed the unstable silt-laden upper waters into Lake Wahapo. Fishing subsequently improved, as the middle and lower reaches drain swampland and seldom discolour. This stable, clear river meandering through swampy cattle country offers excellent fly fishing for large brown trout. Fish can readily be spotted and stalked in the long glides, but a careful approach is necessary for success. The banks are reasonably clear but there are patches of bush, toitoi and scrub.

The river has a sand and shingle bed, offers plenty of fishable water, and is highly recommended to fly anglers. Try Greenwell's Glory, Twilight Beauty and Dad's Favourite dry flies along with Perla, Hare and Copper and Stonefly nymphs.

Lake Wahapo

Location   S.H.6 follows the southern shore of this lake south of Whataroa.

Season   Open all year.

Lake Wahapo contains browns best fished for from a boat. The lake often tends to be silt-laden from water entering from the upper reaches of the Waitangitaona River, and is therefore not greatly recommended.

Lake Mapourika

Location and access   Lies 10 km north of Franz Josef. S.H.6 follows along the eastern shoreline and there are boat-launching facilities at the southern end of the lake.

Season   1 September–30 April for trout, 1 September–31 March for salmon. Fishing in McDonalds Creek is not permitted.

Restrictions   Only 1 salmon may be taken per day on a single hook; the size limit is 30 cm.

This is an excellent lake, holding good-sized browns and a small population of resident quinnat salmon first released into the lake in 1932. In February and March, a run of quinnat enters the lake up the Okarito River from the sea. There are a few selected shoreline spots where one can fly fish, but the prime position is at the mouth of McDonalds Creek and the outlet of the Okarito River. Although the lake water is peat-stained, fish can be spotted and stalked in this area, especially early in the season when the lake is low. A boat or float tube is a decided advantage, however, as most fish are caught by trolling a spinner or spin fishing from the shore.

Shoreline fly fishing is difficult in most places due to overhanging bush. The mouth of Red Jacks Creek on the eastern side of the lake is another top spot. A few salmon up to 6 kg are caught each year on deeply trolled spinners and by threadline anglers fishing the mouth of McDonalds Creek. Anglers using flies for trout should try Coch-y-bondhu, Royal Wulff or Black Gnat dry flies and Orange Rabbit, Hamill's Killer or a smelt pattern such as Grey Ghost and Yellow Dorothy lures.

The Okarito River holds fish but is generally swift, tea-coloured, overgrown by bush and difficult. The road to Okarito crosses the river near The Forks and S.H.6 follows the true right bank upstream for some distance. There are some deep, slow-flowing stretches alongside S.H.6 that are well worth investigating. Try either a spinner or a sunk lure fished across and down if you can find room to cast.

Docherty Creek just south of Franz Josef and Mahitahi River at Bruce Bay hold browns but are not highly recommended as both are flood-prone and unstable.

Jacobs River (Makawhio)

Location and access   Drains the Main Divide and enters the sea at Makawhio Point just north of Bruce Bay. At Jacobs River where S.H.6 crosses there is a side road upstream from the school on the southern side of the bridge. This crosses private farmland to a locked gate. The present landowner lives at Fox Glacier.

Season   1 October–30 April.

This is an excellent river holding good-sized browns. The middle reaches are clear, slow flowing and difficult to fish for this reason, but trout are easy to spot. If one is prepared to tramp upstream for 5 km into the bush, there is good water for fly and spin fishing in the gorge. The river is clear and wadable but rises alarmingly during nor'west rain. There is a good 6 km of fishing water for the tramper/angler; one of my hunting friends has frequently varied his venison diet with trout caught from this river on threadline gear. Large sea-run browns are taken from the lower reaches in the whitebait season, usually on spinners.

Paringa River

Location and access   S.H.6 crosses this river just north of Lake Paringa.

Season   1 October–31 May.

The Paringa is a flood-prone, unstable, shingly river, yet it holds a few brown trout. Sea-run fish enter the river early in the season, chasing whitebait, and the more stable upper reaches are worth exploring for the tramper/angler. The best stretch of water is downstream from S.H.6 to the confluence of Hall River.

The tea-coloured Hall River draining Lake Paringa and joining the Paringa River is well worth exploring, but a good 5 km walk is required to reach the confluence. Quinnat salmon can be caught below the confluence late in the season.

Lake Paringa

Location and access   S.H.6 runs along the south-eastern shore of this lake, which lies between Bruce Bay and Haast. Basic camping facilities are available.

Season   1 October–31 May.

This lake holds brown trout averaging 1.5 kg, with a small run of quinnat salmon entering the lake via Hall River from March to May. These spawn in Windbag Creek, which is closed to fishing. It's best fished from a boat by trolling a spinner. The shore is difficult to fish, being swampy and bush-covered to the water's edge. However, there are places where spinning gear can be used. The mouth of Collie Creek in the south arm is a favourite location, though access is only by boat.

Lake Moeraki

Location and access   Lies closer to the sea than Lake Paringa and 15 km further south on S.H.6.

Season   1 September–31 May.

Restrictions   The Moeraki (Blue) River, which enters the top end of Lake Moeraki, is closed to fishing because of spawning salmon.

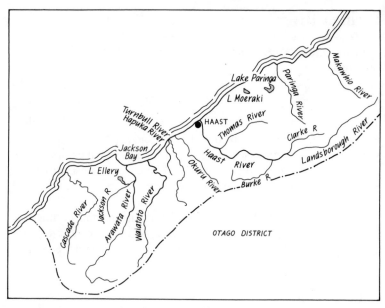

West Coast District (southern section)

The lake is surrounded by bush and swamp so shoreline fishing is difficult, especially when the lake is high. However, shoreline fishing is possible along the eastern shore and around the delta of the Moeraki River. Fish can be seen cruising this area and will accept a small dry fly or nymph provided the deception is cast well ahead of the fish. Boat fishing, either fly casting or trolling, is most popular as there are plenty of good-sized brown trout in this lake. A few quinnat salmon also enter the lake in February–April to spawn in the Moeraki River.

I crossed the upper reaches of the Moeraki as a teenager when tramping from Paringa to Makarora on the Paringa–Haast cattle track before the Haast Pass road had been constructed, and the river was full of trout. Apparently, helicopters now transport anglers to the upper reaches despite the restriction on fishing. The peat-stained Maori River entering the Waita holds good fish, but this is only of interest to trampers.

Haast River and tributaries

Season   1 September–31 May.

Haast River

Location and access This large, snow-fed river drains an extensive
area of the Southern Alps and enters the sea near the township
of Haast. S.H.6 follows the river upstream from where it crosses
at Haast and access is not difficult from this road.

The middle and lower reaches may hold fish, but the river is very
large, unstable and flood-prone and holds glacial silt. Upstream from
the Clarke Bluff where the Clarke and Landsborough tributaries join,
there is more confined, stable water suitable for spinning. However,
despite the scenic qualities of the river in this stretch, fish stocks are
not high. Above the Burke tributary, the water becomes boisterous
and difficult.

Thomas River

Location Flows on a south-westerly course through virgin and
remote mountainous country to join the Haast River on the true
right bank about 12 km upriver from Haast township opposite
Thomas Bluff.

Access The Haast River presents a formidable barrier to cross
at this point and generally a boat must be used. Floods are very
common in this area of high rainfall. There's a good 6-bunk hut
in the Thomas Valley about 6 km from the confluence with the
Haast and an overgrown track up the true left bank. It's a three-
hour tramp to the hut. The safest entry to the valley is by helicopter.
It's possible to tramp from the S.H.6 bridge over the Haast to the
Haast–Thomas confluence, but there is no track.

This is an excellent remote river holding browns up to 3.5 kg in clear
water. Floods can be frightening in this valley as the river can rise
4–5 m at the hut. The best water lies two hours' tramp upstream from
the hut, where there are well-defined pools and runs holding large
fish. Near the hut, the river is full of logs and stumps and the water
is deep and slow flowing. Downstream from the hut lies an impressive
rugged gorge that is not worth fishing. Towards the confluence with
the Haast there are some large pools holding trout. Anglers are strongly
recommended to follow catch and release methods as the fishery could
become fragile if over-fished. Sandfly and mosquito protection is

essential; it's necessary to keep the fire going all night in the hut to prevent a mosquito invasion down the chimney!

The remote Thomas River. Guess where the trout go when hooked!

Clarke River

> **Location and access**   Joins the Landsborough 5 km upstream from Clarke Bluff and enters the parent river at this point. Access is not easy and the Landsborough River must be crossed. In low water conditions an experienced party may be able to ford below Strutt Bluff. However, the Landsborough is a major obstacle and should be treated with great respect.

Angling here is best combined with tramping. The lower reaches are braided, shingly and unstable, but 10 km upstream in the area round Rabbit Flat there is limited boots-and-shorts, back-country fishing for a few brown trout in clear water.

Landsborough River

This is the largest tributary of the Haast, being over 50 km in length, and drains the glaciers and snowfields of the Main Divide. The glacial water is blue-grey in colour and not very clear. Trampers, mountaineers and rafters frequent this remote valley, and though this boisterous, flood-prone river undoubtedly holds fish it cannot be recommended.

Burke River

This rough, gorgy and rocky river joins the Haast in the upper reaches 10 km upstream from Clarke Bluff on S.H.6. A tramping track follows the true left bank upstream, although anglers often use helicopters for transport. This river offers good back-country fishing in remote, heavily bushed, high-rainfall country. Anglers visiting the area should be experienced trampers. Catch and release recommended. The Wills River joins the Haast at the Gates of Haast but is not worth fishing.

Okuru River

> **Location and access**   Drains the Browning and Mark ranges south of Haast River, flows north-west eventually across farmland and enters a lagoon just west of the Haast Motor Camp. The upper reaches can be reached by tramping or by helicopter. Franklin Hut is a good base but is a very full day's tramp from the road end. Nolan's Road on the true left bank leads to good water in the lower reaches.
>
> **Season**   1 September–31 May.

The upper reaches offer excellent remote brown trout fishing in clear mountain water. Fish are easily spotted in clear pools, but catch and release is recommended, especially for those anglers flying in. The lower reaches provide long glides, willow-lined banks and a shingle bed where trout can also be spotted.

Turnbull River

> **Location and access**   Rises from similar bush-clad, mountainous country as the Okuru River, flows parallel to, but south of, the Okuru and enters the same estuary. There are roads up both banks of the lower reaches, which leave the Haast–Jackson Bay road in the vicinity of the Haast Motor Camp.

There are no trout above the power station in Venture Gorge. Across the farmland, there are long willow-lined pools and clear water carrying a good stock of brown trout. Walk across the paddocks at the Haast Gun Club off the north bank road. The river is somewhat flood-prone, but the riverbed is shingly and stable. Sunken logs and snags provide help to hooked fish.

Hapuka River

Location and access   This tea-coloured, slow-flowing river drains swampland south of the Turnbull River and again enters the same estuary. Walk across the paddocks opposite the Okuru venison factory.

The banks of this river are swampy and difficult and the river is best fished with threadline gear. At least one local angler drift fishes down the river in a boat with good results, especially early in the season when whitebait are running. Try Yellow Dorothy, Grey Ghost, Yellow Rabbit and Doll Fly. Any silver or gold spinner will be effective.

Waiatoto River

Location and access   The Jackson Bay road crosses upstream from the mouth.

This is a large, glacial and snow-fed river rising from Mt Aspiring and entering the sea 12 km south of Okuru. Although the river holds fish and has a reasonably stable bed, only the estuary and lower reaches can be recommended. Early in the season, during the whitebait run, there are excellent sea-run or estuarine brown trout to be caught. Access is difficult, however, as the road downstream on the true left bank only goes as far as Hindley Creek. A jet boat is the answer! Hindley Creek itself holds brown trout. Use threadline gear or a smelt fly on a sinking line. For the tramper/angler, the Te Naihi tributary at Axius Flats, the Drake at Drake Flats and the upper reaches around Bonar Flats are worth exploring with a spinner.

Arawata River

Access   The road to Jackson Bay crosses upstream from the mouth at the confluence of the Jackson River. A jet boat also provides the best means of transport on this river, although the mouth can be reached by walking north along Neils Beach. Watch for dive-bombing Caspian terns during the nesting season!

Season   1 September–31 May.

The Arawata is another large, glacier-fed river flowing parallel to, but south of, the Waiatoto. However, it's far more unstable, flood-prone and shingly than the Waiatoto River and generally holds glacial flour. Rarely does it become clear, but when it does there is good spin fishing near the bridge for large sea-run browns during the whitebait migration from September to January. The headwaters of the Arawata hold a few brown trout, but only the hunter or tramper would bother with fishing in this remote high-rainfall country.

Jackson River

Location and access   Drains the McArthur Tops and Lake Ellery and joins the Arawata near the Jackson Road bridge. The Jackson River road to Cascade follows up the river. This road is rough in parts, with fords, and is most suitable for four-wheel-drive vehicles.

The Jackson is a pleasant rock and stone river overhung by bush in parts and holding a few large brown trout, though not in great numbers. The water is clear above the Ellery confluence but becomes slightly tea-coloured below. It's best fished below the confluence, where trout numbers are greater.

Many years ago I landed a 4 kg fish on a Willesden Green minnow but not without a struggle, as the fish raced downstream to bury itself in the usual hide of dead trees. Chest deep in water, I managed to free the fish and then had to compete with a large eel. I rescued the fish and lived to tell the tale!

Lake Ellery

Access   It is a 40-minute walk on a marked track up the outlet stream from the Jackson River road to this attractive lake encircled by dense bush.

Season   1 September–31 May.

This peat-stained scenic lake is difficult to fish from shore. A jet boat or rubber dinghy should be launched below the bridge on the Jackson River road and near the Jackson River confluence. There is only one stretch of the Ellery River that is shallow. Brown trout can be stalked in the shallows near the outlet when the lake is low. Otherwise, the lake is best fished with a spinner. Trout in this lake feed on fresh water mussels. A smaller edition of the Crested Grebe, the Dabchick, resides on the waters of this lake. The heavily peat-stained Ellery River is worth a cast or two with a spinner.

Martyr River

Location and access   Drains the northern end of the bush-clad Olivine Range, flows in a northerly direction and joins the Cascade River 3 km west of the site of the old Martyr Homestead. The lower end of the Jackson River road follows the true left bank downstream. Access below the road end is across farmland.

There are no trout above Monkey Puzzle Gorge. Below the gorge, the river is shingly and flood-prone, but the confluence with the Cascade and the lower 2 km of river is well worth fishing. It's an hour's walk from the road end across swampy farmland to the confluence. The water is clear and fish are easily spotted.

Cascade River

Location and access   This remote river, draining the Olivine Range and the Red Hills, flows north to The Bend near Smiths Ponds, then turns to the north-west and enters the sea 20 km south of Jackson Bay. Take the Jackson River road to the Martyr Homestead (now burned down and replaced by a small house) in the lower reaches. The upper reaches can only be reached by the tramper.

The lower 18 km below the Martyr River confluence is tidal and swampy but supports the largest whitebait population in New Zealand. There are plenty of fish in these reaches, especially in the pool at the Martyr confluence. A rubber dinghy is an advantage. Use a smelt fly or a silver or gold spinner during the whitebait season. Upstream this river offers superb brown trout fishing for the adventurous and fit tramper/angler, especially up through and above the Cascade Gorge where large browns can be spotted and stalked in clear pools and runs. There are no tracks or huts above The Bend.

The inaccessible Gorge River between the Cascade and Big Bay holds a few brown trout in the lower reaches only.

North Canterbury District

This large and varied district stretches from the Conway River in the north-east to the Rakaia River in the south-east; from Lake Tennyson in the north-west to Arthurs Pass and the Rakaia headwaters in the south-west. In the west lie the Southern Alps and foothills rising to over 2 000 m. The intensely farmed and fertile Canterbury Plains stretch from these foothills to the Pacific Ocean on the east coast. The strong prevailing westerly winds often play havoc with angling intentions. These winds collect moisture from the Tasman Sea and, as the airstream rises and cools, dump most of this water on the West Coast and Southern Alps. The resulting strong, warm nor'wester then sweeps down the Canterbury Plains, drying all before it.

An angler can leave Christchurch on a calm morning intent on fishing a high-country lake only to have these plans dashed by a nor'wester. These strong winds usually precede a low pressure centre and a cold front, so visiting anglers should beware of the weather, especially in spring; not only is casting into the wind impossible, but you can hardly stand upright in a good blow! Don't leave Christchurch for the high-country unless there is calm anticyclonic weather or a moderate easterly or sou'westerly blowing.

This weather pattern in summer can also adversely affect some fishing waters. With low rainfall, high temperatures and nor'westerly weather, rain-fed streams crossing the plains dry rapidly or disappear beneath their shingle bed. Salvage operations to rescue stranded fish are all part of the job for the North Canterbury Fish and Game Council. Rivers commonly affected include the Ashley, Selwyn, Hororata and Hawkins.

Quinnat salmon run up most of the snow-fed rivers, which do not dry to the same extent, the Rakaia, Waimakariri and Hurunui offering most sport from late January to April. There are brown and rainbow trout throughout this district, a few macinaw in Lake Pearson and landlocked quinnat salmon in Lake Coleridge.

> **Season**   Unless otherwise stated, 1 October–30 April for waters other than the high-country lakes. For these lakes: the first Saturday in November–30 April. There's a winter extension to the season for certain waters – from the first Saturday after Queen's Birthday Weekend to 31 August.
>
> **Restrictions**   The bag limit is 14 trout or salmon; minimum length 25 cm. Only 10 quinnat salmon or trout may be taken from Lake Coleridge; 4 quinnat salmon from any other water.

Conway River

> **Location and access**   Rises in the Seaward Kaikoura Range, flows in a south-easterly direction and enters the sea east of Hundalee. Access can be obtained from S.H.1 at Hundalee, although a small shingle road to Ferniehurst leads to better water.

The Conway is not highly recommended as it's very prone to flooding and changing course. It does hold a few small brown trout in the more stable gorge pools for those prepared to walk the shingle riverbed, and there are some sea-run trout at the mouth.

Lake Tennyson

> **Location and access**   This lake lies in the headwaters of the Clarence River beneath the Spenser Mountains. Take the road from Hanmer over Jacks Pass to the Clarence River. Proceed upstream on this metalled hydro road and cross the upper reaches of the Clarence River downstream from the outlet. Soon after this crossing, a track leads off to the left to the south end of the lake. There's easy walking right round this high-country lake, and camping is permitted.

This lake contains brown trout in the 1–1.5 kg range. Both the outlet and the top end of the lake where the river flows in are good spots. Fish can be taken on a fly or spinner and stalked round the tussock and shingle shore in bright conditions. Try Twilight Beauty, Black Gnat or Love's Lure. The nor'wester whistles down this lake and it should only be visited in high summer. In winter, the mountains are snow-covered and the area becomes very desolate and inhospitable.

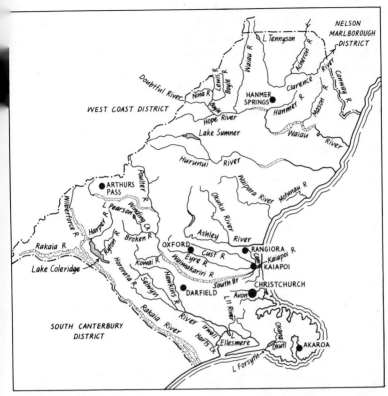

North Canterbury District

Clarence River

Location   Drains the Molesworth country and the Spenser Mountains. Flows into and out of Lake Tennyson in a south-easterly direction to just north of Hanmer. Here it changes direction to the north-east and flows through a series of deep gorges in rugged, inaccessible country between the Inland and Seaward Kaikoura Mountains, finally entering the Pacific Ocean 40 km north of Kaikoura. The lower reaches are not worth fishing.

Access   Take the Jacks Pass road from Hanmer to the metalled hydro road. This follows the river upstream to well beyond Lake Tennyson and downstream to the confluence with the Acheron.

Restrictions   The bag limit for the river and its tributaries is 2 fish.

The best water lies across the tussock flats off the Hanmer hydro road described above. The upper reaches of this river below Lake Tennyson flow down a wide, exposed valley often swept by nor'westers. However, in the calm, bright conditions that occasionally prevail, good browns up to 2.5 kg can be spotted and stalked with a dry fly or nymph. Fish stocks are not high, but the trout are generally well worth catching. There are attractive pools and runs across a stone and rock bed and plenty of water to walk and fish. Trout can also be taken on spinners. There are fish below the Acheron confluence, but access is very limited unless the river is rafted or tramped. The remote middle and lower reaches are gorgy, unstable, shingly and prone to discolouration and silting during a fresh.

Acheron River

Location and access   This major tributary of the Clarence flows south from Molesworth to join the Clarence north of Hanmer. Take the Jacks Pass road and turn downstream until the bridge over the Clarence to the Acheron Valley is reached. Sometimes there is a chain over this bridge preventing access, but recently this has been removed. The road follows up the true right bank.

Nymphing the high-country Doubtful River.

This is a similar river to the upper Clarence, requiring similar fishing methods. There's good spotting for browns up to 3 kg, but they are wary. It's boots-and-shorts fishing. Again, the main obstacle on this river is the prevailing downstream nor'wester, so it pays to carry a sinking line and a few lures in case upstream fishing becomes impossible. Catch and release recommended.

Waiau River and tributaries

Waiau River

Location   Rises in the Lewis Pass and Spenser Mountains. The main tributaries join the Upper Waiau at Glenhope. The river then parallels S.H.7 almost to Culverden before turning to the north-east, entering the sea just north of Cheviot.

Access   *Upper Waiau*
- Permission must be obtained from St James Station in the Clarence Valley before crossing Malings Pass into the Upper Waiau from the Hanmer Springs hydro road. There is four-wheel-drive access over Malings Pass and also over private land via the Edwards River to the south.
- Trampers can reach the river in two days via the St James Walkway starting from Lewis Pass and up Cannibal Gorge on the Maruia River, or alternatively up the Boyle River at the other end of the Walkway. The Christopher Hut on the Ada and the Tin Jug Hut at the mouth of Steyning Stream provide good shelter.

Middle and lower reaches   No problems with road access off S.H.7 or the Rotherham–Waiau road.

Season   There's a winter extension below the Hope River.

The best fly water is on the upper reaches flowing through the old Ada Station on the St James Walkway, where fish up to 4.5 kg can be spotted and stalked in clear pools and runs. The river winds across a tussock valley fringed with bush, and near the old Ada Station there is a deep, unfishable gorge with good pools at either end. Wild cherries and gooseberries grow near the Ada Station and these provided a fitting close to a meal I once shared with two deerstalkers and a friend. The first course was a 4.6 kg brown trout caught by my friend on an eelskin minnow.

The middle and lower reaches are large, shingly and unstable, and the brown trout present are mainly caught on spinning gear by salmon anglers. A good run of quinnat salmon occurs in this river from February to April.

There are brown trout in Lake Guyon to be found close to the true left bank of the Upper Waiau, upstream from the Ada River confluence, and a four-wheel-drive vehicle is useful for access.

All the tributaries contain good-sized brown trout in clear mountain water. They are boots-and-shorts rivers where fishing should be combined with tramping. Remember, this is high mountain country with unpredictable weather patterns. Fish readily accept weighted nymphs and well-hackled dry flies carefully presented. Don't neglect the fast pocket water in summer. Polaroids are essential for spotting if fly fishing.

Nina River

Location and access   You must either cross by wire or ford the Lewis River to reach the Nina. Access off S.H.7 about 1 km upstream of the confluence of the Nina and Lewis rivers near Palmer Lodge, the New Zealand Deerstalkers' Association Hut. A track then crosses the strip of land between the two rivers and leads to the Nina on the true right bank of the Lewis.

A typical high-country rock and stone river, the Nina flows across bush-fringed grassy flats. Though it doesn't hold a lot of fish, those there are are well worth catching.

Boyle River

Access   Off S.H.7 at the Boyle settlement and the marked St James Walkway. There's a four-wheel-drive track to St Andrews in the Magdalene Valley.

There are good pools and runs to explore on this river, especially where the Walkway leaves the river for some distance. This clear, vigorous mountain stream, flowing through beech bush and holding a reasonable number of fish, is recommended to the fly angler who isn't afraid to walk and who enjoys stalking trout in a back-country river.

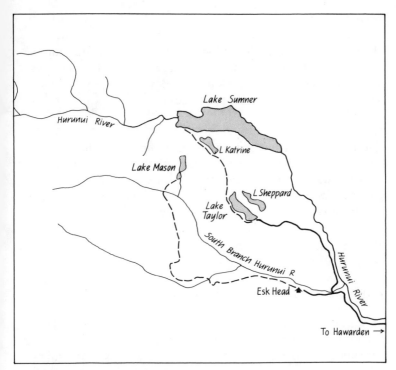

Lake Sumner Forest Park

Doubtful River

Location and access   Rises near the Amuri Pass and flows in an easterly direction to join the Lewis on its true right bank 5 km south of the Boyle confluence. Access off S.H.7.

The Doubtful is a good high-country river with fast, clear, broken water holding good brown trout, but tramping experience is recommended. Grassy flats and bush line the banks. Shelter is available at the Doubtful Hut about 6 km upstream near the mouth of Devilskin Stream. Fishing is good for 5–6 km up this river.

Lewis River

The Lewis flows alongside S.H.7 but is steep and rough and the fishing water is severely limited. Perhaps it is worth a brief look during low-water summer conditions.

Hope River

Location and access   The Hope River track to the Hurunui and Harper Pass follows up this river. Access is off S.H.7 3 km west of Poplars Station at a car-park near the Boyle River. A swingbridge just upstream from the car-park marks the start of the track at Windy Point.

This river is rather unstable and prone to flooding. There are good fish in the gorge above the confluence with the Kiwi Stream, but this is a day's walk from S.H.7. I once sheltered in a small tent during a spectacular electrical storm and watched the river rise alarmingly fast. Even the Kiwi Stream was waist deep and difficult to ford.

There are only a few fish in the Mason River, which follows S.H.70 north of Waiau township.

Lake Sumner Forest Park

Location   The Park covers 74 000 ha of mountains, forests, lakes and rivers. Permits are only required for hunting and there's good accommodation in 18 Parks Board huts. Camping is also permitted. Anglers visiting the Park for the first time are advised to obtain a detailed map from the Department of Survey and Land Information (NZMS 1: S 53). There are a number of four-wheel-drive tracks in this area, but most are over private land adjoining the Park.

Access
- Take the road to Hawarden off S.H.7 at Waikari, then the road to Lake Sumner. Don't go beyond Lake Taylor unless your vehicle is four-wheel-drive, in which case you can reach the No. 2 hut at the head of Lake Sumner some 20 km further on.
- Tramp the Hope Valley from the Lewis Pass road, or from the West Coast via the Taramakau River Valley and Harper Pass.

Season   First Saturday in November–30 April. There's a winter extension to the season from the first Saturday after Queen's Birthday to 31 August for Lakes Sumner and Taylor only.

Restrictions   Mechanically powered boats are only permitted on Lake Sumner. Non-mechanically propelled boats are permitted

> elsewhere in these high-country lakes. Fly fishing only permitted in Lake Sheppard.

Lake Sumner contains brown and rainbow trout, and quinnat salmon also run into this lake from the Hurunui River. The other lakes (Taylor, Sheppard, Katrine and Mason) hold brown trout only. Sumner, the largest lake, covering 1 364 ha, is best fished from a boat either trolling a spinner or harling a fly, but the catch rate is not high.

Trout can be spotted in all the lakes cruising the shoreline and respond to small, unweighted nymphs fished on a floating line, dry flies such as Coch-y-bondhu, Black Gnat, Red Palmer and Mole Fly, and lures of the bully variety such as Muddler Minnow, Lord's Killer, Mrs Simpson, Hamill's Killer and Rabbit flies. An imitation cicada or cricket can be deadly. There's good spinning from the shore in all lakes except Lake Sheppard, which is reserved for fly fishing. Lake Mason is the most remote lake but can be reached by tramping for a couple of hours from the Lake Sumner Hut at the head of Lake Sumner or by four-wheel-drive. Fish average 1.3–1.5 kg. Watch out for cruising eels in Lake Sheppard – I had one round my bare leg when wading in sandshoes and shorts – a most unnerving experience! There's plenty of water to fish in most attractive remote surroundings and the Park offers tramping, deerstalking, pig hunting and swimming during high summer.

Hurunui River

Location   Saddles with the Taramakau River at Harper Pass and flows into and out of Lake Sumner. Side streams drain the Nelson Tops. Flows generally north-east from the outlet of Lake Sumner to reach S.H.7 at Hurunui on the edge of Balmoral Forest, is crossed by S.H.1 at Greta Paddock, and enters the sea at Hurunui Mouth south of Cheviot.

Access
Upper reaches   From the Lake Sumner road.

Middle and lower reaches   From S.H.7 and S.H.1 and side roads off these highways.

Season   A winter extension applies below the south branch junction.

The best trout fishing water is in the upper reaches off the Lake Sumner road and above the Mandamus confluence. Walk down to the river from where this road leaves the river at Surveyors Stream. The river is stable and flows through a succession of short, attractive gorges. Because it drains Lake Sumner, the water remains reasonably clear even in a fresh. This 10 km of highly regarded heavy water downstream from the outlet of Sumner is clear, is accessible to the fit angler and holds an excellent stock of mainly brown trout up to 3.5 kg in deep pools and swift runs (more than 50 large fish/km on drift dives). These fish respond to large buoyant dry flies, well-weighted nymphs and spinners. For a surprise, there is an occasional rainbow.

Below the Mandamus, the river holds a few trout in deep holes and gorges but becomes a large braided river in the lower reaches and is more suited to spinning. There are good salmon runs into the mouth, a favourite spot for the spin angler.

Hurunui tributaries

Two are worthy of fishing, especially early in the season when waterflows are consistent. Brown trout can be spotted and stalked with dry fly or nymph. These are:

Pahau River

Crosses S.H.7 just south of Culverden. Take the road from Culverden to Pahau Downs. The Pahau Ford road also crosses the river. The Pahau used to dry in summer but is now supplemented by irrigation water and holds small brown trout.

Waitohi River

From Hurunui on S.H.7 proceed to Horsely Downs. Medbury and Bakers roads lead to the river. This is a small, shingly stream holding fish averaging 0.75–1 kg, but the river tends to dry in summer, so it's best fished early in the season.

The Motunau River at Motunau Beach contains small brown trout and some large eels.

Ashley River

> **Location**   Rises from the Puketeraki Range, flows through Lees Valley and the Ashley Gorge, then turns north-east and flows across the plains just north of Rangiora to reach the sea at Waikuku Beach.

The Ashley holds limited stocks of smallish brown trout which I have yet to encounter. There are well-defined pools and runs in the gorge, but on the day I fished through it a savage nor'wester whipped up stones and dust and blew my well-weighted nymph back down the line. However, a young angler did land a nice 1.5 kg fish on a spinner from a pool at the top of the gorge as I arrived. There's great swimming and picnicking at Ashley Gorge, but that hardly helps the angler. Across the plains the river is unstable in a fresh and often dries during summer. Again it's best fished early in the season. Quinnat salmon spawn in the upper reaches above the gorge.

The Okuku tributary at White Rock and Lees Pass holds a few browns for the tramper/angler entering the Mt Thomas State Forest Park.

Waimakariri River and tributaries

Waimakariri River

Middle and lower reaches   S.H.1 crosses the river between Belfast and Kaiapoi. Roads follow upstream on either bank, although in some stretches they are a good distance from the river.

Mouth   At Kairaki.

Season   Winter extension below white posts at Woodstock.

Because of shifting shingle and floods this river does not provide good trout habitat, but there are some large browns in the gorge and upper reaches, where the river tends to be more stable. As a keen teenager I tramped across Flock Hill Station to the river behind the Craigieburn Railway Station and found some good fish, although access to the river was very limited. A jet boat is the answer! I well remember two large brown trout shot with a speargun by two farmhands beneath the Mt White bridge. The station owner, their employer, was not amused.

The river is more suited to spinning than fly fishing although a few hardy anglers braving the nor'westers have favoured spots which yield fish to the fly. The lower end of the Bealey usually holds the odd trout. The pools often change from year to year. Unfortunately the lower reaches below S.H.1 have been polluted in the past and hold few trout. The river is heavily fished by salmon anglers, however.

Among the tributaries of the Waimakariri, four can be recommended, though there are a few fish in some of the others, such as the Hawdon, generally visited by tramper/anglers. Lake Minchin at the head of the Poulter River holds trout, but again this is only of interest to trampers. In the lower reaches near Kaiapoi, Rangiora and Belfast, the Kaiapoi, Cam, Cust, Silverstream and Styx tributaries all hold small trout, but pollution and water extraction is a problem in all these streams and they are not greatly recommended.

Poulter River

Location and access   Drains the Dampier, Poulter and Savannah ranges, flows in a southerly direction and joins the Waimakariri River near Whale Hill. Access from the Mt White road which crosses the lower reaches. Tramping experience required to reach the middle and upper reaches.

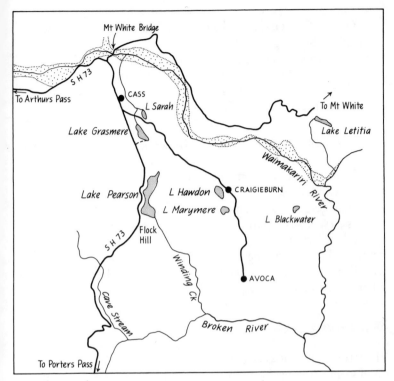

Lake Pearson and adjacent lakes

The lower reaches are unstable and flood-prone. There's good back-country fishing for browns in the east branch as far up as Cox River and in the west branch upstream from the east branch confluence. Quinnat salmon spawn in the river late in the season. The stream draining into the Poulter from Lake Minchin does not restock the lake.

Broken River

Location   Rises in the Craigieburn Range, flows in a north-easterly direction and joins the Waimakariri near Staircase. The Thomas and Porter rivers join opposite Castle Hill to form Broken River. One small tributary near Castle Hill, Cave Stream, runs underground through a limestone cave.

Access
- Through private land at Flock Hill Station by following down

Winding Creek to its confluence with Broken River. The present runholder charges for this access.
- S.H.73 crosses the upper reaches near Castle Hill. You can walk downstream if energetic, though the river is flanked by limestone cliffs for the first few kilometres. It's 15 km to the Winding Creek confluence.

This river holds both rainbow and brown trout, but fish numbers are not great; if you spot three or four fish per kilometre you're doing well. Some fish are very difficult to see in the white water during hot summer conditions. The river, cutting through open tussock country and rough gorges, is small, rocky, boisterous and fast-flowing but easy to cross, especially above the Winding Creek confluence. All fly methods and spinning will take fish but catch and release should be practised. Below Winding Creek the water often carries silt, and fish are difficult to spot, but rainbows will take a lure of the Rabbit variety when fished deeply through the holes.

Winding Creek

Location   Drains Lake Pearson when the lake is sufficiently high and swampland on Flock Hill Station. Flows south-west through tussock and scrub to join Broken River about 8 km above Staircase.

Access   By permission of the runholder at Flock Hill Station; a farm track leads close to the river some 4 km from the homestead.

This narrow, deep stream holds good fish, mainly rainbow, in pools and runs, though in places the stream is overgrown with manuka and matagouri and difficult to fish. Try weighted nymphs and be prepared to lose fish as they tear off downstream. This is a very important salmon spawning stream for the Waimakariri.

The South Branch

Location   Located close to Christchurch just north of Belfast, the stream flows north-east through orchards and farmland to join the Waimakariri near the roadbridge on S.H.1. The riverbed is an old river channel of the Waimakariri.

This is ideal water for young Christchurch anglers to learn the art of fly fishing. It is a very testing stream, as I well remember from my school days, when I first learned that an evening rise had nothing to do with the opposite sex! The first kilometre upstream from where it enters the Waimakariri has been ruined by freezing works and effluent discharge and is now a mud drain. Fortunately the freezing works discharges have now ceased. Above this stretch the river is spring-fed and clear and flows over a shingle and weed bed where fish can be spotted. The occasional reach is choked with willows, but the stream offers interesting fly fishing for small brown trout in the 0.5–1 kg range.

The river is well stocked, there's a good evening rise, and the stream can be waded in thigh boots. The most popular stretch of water is from the raupo below the Dickeys Road bridge to the Groynes picnic area. Use small, lightly weighted nymphs during the day and a Twilight

Nestled in a tussock and matagouri basin, Lake Pearson holds mackinaw.

97

Beauty in the evening. If the fish rise madly and ignore your dry fly try a sparsely hackled wet fly or small sedge fished upstream.

The Avon River and its small, spring-fed tributaries, the Waimari and Wairarapa streams, flowing through the suburbs of Christchurch, hold reasonable stocks of small brown trout offering sport to junior anglers.

North Canterbury high-country lakes

Lake Lyndon

> **Location and access**   Reached from S.H.73 near the top of Porters Pass.

Lyndon is an exposed high-country lake surrounded by barren tussock terrain and overstocked with small rainbow trout. Fish are difficult to spot but will take flies or spinners when fishing blind. Easy access and safe wading.

Lyndon Tarn

On the back road from Lake Lyndon to Lake Coleridge, this tarn has a rather swampy, willow-lined shore and holds small rainbow.

Lake Pearson

> **Location and access**   On S.H.73 just north of Flock Hill Station on the way to Arthurs Pass.

The lake is shaped like an hour-glass and holds brown and rainbow trout along with a few macinaw (North American char), which have not done very well in the past, though there was another release in 1988. Macinaw seldom grow beyond 1 kg in this lake and are rather disappointing to catch. The lake lies in a tussock and matagouri basin and has easy shoreline access with only a few willows in selected spots. Fish can be spotted in clear conditions and will accept Coch-y-bondhu, Pevril o' the Peak, Red Tipped Governor, Black Gnat and Palmer dry flies, or size 8 Hamill's Killer and Mrs Simpson lures. An imitation cicada can bring surprising results. Spinning methods will also take fish, with flatfish and a dark cobra being useful. The 'Narrows', close to the main road, is a good place to spot fish. The Grasmere end of the lake, where it is safe to wade, is also a favoured spot, especially in a nor'wester as the offshore wind will blow from behind. At times the wind can be so strong that it becomes unnecessary to cast — just hold your rod in the air, pay out line and gently lower!

Lake Grasmere

Location and access   A few kilometres beyond Lake Pearson, a small vehicle track off S.H.73 leads to a campsite on the shore of this attractive lake.

Most of the shoreline is swampy though generally negotiable in sandshoes. The rocky north-west shore is backed by a steep bush-covered hill. Lake Grasmere holds rainbow and browns averaging around 1–2 kg. Unfortunately the water quality in this lake has deteriorated over the years because of farm run-off through the swamp and a high population of bird life in this wildlife refuge. However, it's still a very productive and pleasant lake to fish.

Trout can still be spotted cruising the shoreline in good conditions and respond to the same flies as suggested for Lake Pearson. The outlet stream at the northern end of the lake holds fish but is overgrown and difficult. As a young teenager I witnessed an angler hook and land a 3.5 kg rainbow on a Pevril o' the Peak dry fly. The power of that fish left such a deep impression on me that I became frightened to fish with my grossly inadequate bamboo rod and Nottingham reel.

Lake Sarah

Location and access   On the route to Arthurs Pass between Lake Grasmere and Cass, a metalled road signposted Lake Sarah turns to the right off S.H.73 and crosses the railway line. This leads to Lakes Sarah, Hawdon, Marymere and Blackwater and follows the railway line to Craigieburn Station. Sarah is the first lake reached and is easily seen on the left side of the road.

Sarah holds brown and rainbow with an occasional good fish up to 3.5 kg but most average around the 1.3 kg mark. Fish can be spotted in calm conditions before the nor'wester gets up. Use the same methods as for Lake Pearson, though the swampy and raupo-infested shoreline is more difficult.

Lake Hawdon

Location and access   About 10 km down the Lake Sarah road from where it crosses the railway line, there is a sign indicating a track to Lake Hawdon. It is only a few minutes' walk over the hill to the lake.

Hawdon only holds rainbow trout, but fish up to 2.3 kg can be caught. There is good fly fishing off the beach at the Marymere end of the lake (Lake Marymere is just over the hill) and along the steep south-western shore, where fish can be spotted and stalked from Purple Hill. It pays to have a mate spotting for you up the hillside. Watch the matagouri on the backcast! Cruising fish can be timed on their beat and seem to prefer a small wet fly or unweighted nymph to a dry fly. The swampy northern end has provided me with good fish taken on a spinner. The jacks often have worn-down lower jaws presumably from digging a redd somewhere round the shoreline as there are no spawning streams.

Lake Marymere

Location and access   As mentioned above, this lake lies over a small hill from Hawdon.

Restrictions   Fly fishing only.

Marymere contains only cunning brown trout, some very large. A friend landed a magnificent fish weighing 4.5 kg there three years ago. They are not easy to spot unless conditions are bright. There's an attractive patch of native bush along the south-western shore where I camped on my own for a week as a teenager. Fish can certainly be seen along this rocky shore harvesting nymphs from the crevices. Try Coch-y-bondhu, Love's Lure and Mole Fly dry flies, small lightly weighted nymphs fished on a floating line or bully-type lures such as Muddler Minnow, Lord's Killer and Orange Rabbit fished on a slow-sinking line. Wading is safe.

Lake Blackwater
This tarn lies on Flock Hill Station half way across the tussock flats to the Waimakariri River from Craigieburn Railway Station. Though it does hold rainbows it is not recommended.

Lake Rubicon

This is another small tarn on Brooksdale Station off S.H.73. Turn off onto Brooksdale Road 6 km beyond Springfield and before the climb up to Porters Pass. It's very small and partly surrounded by rushes, and holds rainbow. Years ago they were in poor condition because of parasite infestation, but they have apparently improved recently.

Lake Coleridge

Location   Lies between the Torlesse and Mt Hutt ranges near the Rakaia headwaters (see map).

Access   From Rakaia Gorge take the road to Lake Coleridge on the true left bank of the Rakaia.

Season   First Saturday in November–30 April.

Restrictions   The bag limit is 6 trout or salmon.

This large, cold lake is 18 km long and covers 3 673 ha. It is very exposed to both the nor'wester and the sou'wester and its water level is controlled by a hydro-electric power station. Fluctuating lake levels destroy shoreline food. The lake holds brown and rainbow trout and landlocked quinnat salmon, the latter providing most of the sport. It's a popular fishery, opening day being a ritual observance for some anglers, come hail, rain or snow – the latter being not uncommon. Fish are generally caught by deep trolling a spinner from a boat or spinning from the shore. There's limited shoreline fishing with a sunk lure, but trout are hard to spot so blind fishing is necessary, usually along the eastern shoreline. Fish average 0.75–1.5 kg. Favoured locations include the Harper River diversion and the picket fence at the north end and Ryton Bay on the eastern shore.

The lower reaches of the Ryton, Wilberforce and Harper rivers are spawning grounds and all hold trout, but they are shingly and unstable, and there's minimal bank vegetation and limited holding water, so they are not greatly recommended. These rivers are best fished early in the season as trout tend to return to the lake in warm summer conditions.

There are a number of small lakes scattered around the eastern shore of Lake Coleridge, some of which offer excellent fishing providing

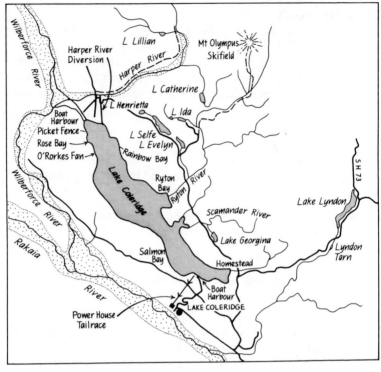

Lake Coleridge and surrounding lakes

the nor'wester doesn't blow you away. In calm, bright conditions, fish can be spotted and stalked as they cruise the shore.

Useful flies include Coch-y-bondhu and Manuka Beetle imitations after Christmas and Black Gnat dry flies, Muddler Minnow and Yellow Rabbit lures and small wet flies such as Twilight Beauty and March Brown for cruising fish ignoring dry flies. Unweighted nymphs are very effective, especially before the green beetle hatch.

Note: The season on these lakes opens on the first Saturday in November and closes on 30 April, except on Lake Selfe, where there is a winter extension to 31 August.

Lake Georgina

Location and access   This is the first lake reached on Harper Road, which skirts the western shore.

Lake Selfe is well known for its large brown trout.

It is a small, exposed lake surrounded by tussock. A row of pine trees provides shelter for basic camping at the northern end. The lake holds rainbow trout, but fish are not easy to spot, though there is easy shoreline access, safe wading and no swamp.

Lake Evelyn

Location and access   Harper Road skirts the western shore after crossing the Ryton River and beyond the junction of the toll road to the Mt Olympus Skifield.

Lake Evelyn holds brown and rainbow trout but is difficult to fish because of swamp and raupo along the shoreline. There are stretches of firm tussock along the northern side, but fish are difficult to spot. Bird life is prolific on this lake, especially Canada geese.

Lake Selfe

Location and access   A few kilometres beyond Lake Evelyn, Harper Road skirts the south-western shore of this lake.

This is the most attractive lake in the area and is well known for its large brown trout, weighing up to 3 kg. Shoreline vegetation includes tussock, matagouri, briar rose and beech trees along the northern shore. The northern end is shallow and cruising fish can be spotted and stalked. Before Christmas, try Black Gnat dry flies, lightly weighted nymphs and Muddler Minnow lures. After Christmas try green beetle imitations, especially along the bush-lined shore. There are basic camping facilities at the southern end.

Lake Henrietta

Location and access   Lies just north of Lake Selfe off the same road.

This very small lake holds large rainbows, but because the shoreline is swampy and infested with flax, scrub and raupo, fishing is not easy. A slowly retrieved lure, perhaps a Mrs Simpson or Kilwell, on a slow-sinking line is as good a method as any.

Lake Ida

Location and access   Lies off the private toll road to the Mt Olympus Skifield.

Ida is a popular ice-skating lake in winter. It lies in a cold, steep-sided basin with tussock and beech trees lining the shore, and supports a stock of small rainbow, as does Little Ida close by.

Lake Catherine (Monck)

Location and access   Lies off the Mt Olympus road with access by four-wheel-drive or on foot.

Surrounded by tussock, matagouri scrub, a few willows and raupo, this lake holds both brown and rainbow trout. Try the mouth of the small stream on the north side, using the same flies as for Lake Selfe.

Lake Lillian, located along the west bank of the Harper River, also holds fish. Access to the fishing huts is by four-wheel-drive.

Okana (Little River) and its tributary the Okuti

Location and access Take S.H.75 from Christchurch to Little River. The Okana drains Little River Valley; the Okuti, the Okuti Valley. The road to Okuti Valley crosses both streams.

These two streams join to form the Takiritawai River just before discharging into the top end of Lake Forsythe near Little River. They have been willow infested in the past and though these have been recently partly cleared, fishing has not improved because of increasing eutrophication in Lake Forsythe. The lower reaches, where most fish are caught, is sluggish, murky and rather unattractive but still yields the odd good-sized fish.

Access is generally easy though the surrounding land is very low lying and gets water-logged when the lake is high. Trout are generally taken during the day on a sunk lure such as Hope's Silvery or a weighted nymph. Most success, however, is achieved by anglers fishing at night with a black night lure such as Hairy Dog, Hope's Dark, Red Shadow or Hart Creek. Use a very slow retrieve and a medium-sinking line. There is a winter extension to the season here.

The Kaituna River, draining the Kaituna Valley and emptying into Lake Ellesmere, is similar in character to the Okana River, and similar fishing methods should be used. The river is crossed by S.H.75 where this highway parallels the lake shore.

Selwyn River

Location Rises from the Big Ben Range and flows east near Glentunnel, Coalgate and Greendale, then across the Canterbury Plains to drain finally into Lake Ellesmere.

Access This is not difficult as there are roads on both sides of the river. There are roads to Selwyn Huts at the mouth, south from Springston, to Chamberlain's and Coe's fords off the Lincoln–Leeston road, and to Glentunnel on the upper reaches. Take the Glentunnel–Whitecliffs road to the Selwyn Gorge.

Season Winter extension downstream from where the South Springston road meets the river. First Saturday after Queen's Birthday Weekend to 31 August.

Lower reaches   This stretch of water has never enticed me as it is slow-flowing, muddy and unattractive. Also the fishing has deteriorated over the last 20 years because of increasing eutrophication in Lake Ellesmere, though good fish are still occasionally taken – generally at night. These are estuarine-living browns from Lake Ellesmere which leave the brackish water and enter the river mouth at night, chasing bullies and smelt. They are taken on a slow-sinking line and lure. The Selwyn mouth has inspired many fly tyers and a number of Canterbury lures originated from this stretch of water. Such lures as Hope's Silvery White and Red, Hope's Dark, Barred Rock and Red Shadow are all still used.

Middle reaches   The river flows over an unstable, willow-lined shingle bed, but water flows in summer are unreliable. The river is often dry at the S.H.1 bridge as the water flows beneath the shingle. Further downstream near Coe's and Chamberlain's fords, there are some good browns in the main holes. These are usually taken at night on a deeply sunk black lure. A student friend told me about poaching here with a speargun; he confirmed that there are indeed some very big trout lying under the banks in the deeper holes. Drift dives have revealed good numbers of fish in the stretch near Coe's Ford (50 fish/km).

Upper reaches   At times there is a reasonable stock of small fish near Glentunnel, but there are few large fish in the Selwyn Gorge (75 fish/km at Whitecliffs, mainly small ones). Fish can occasionally be spotted, however, and will accept dry flies and nymphs. The river is more stable in these areas and there are some good, deep glides under the willows.

There are two tributaries of the Selwyn well worth fishing, especially early in the season before water flows become reduced: these are the Hawkins and Hororata rivers. The Hororata can actually dry up in parts, but in spring, below Hororata township, there is reasonable fishing. The Hawkins can be reached south of Darfield near Greendale while the Hororata can be found at Hororata and Glenroy. Both hold good stocks of brown trout in the 0.75–1.5 kg range with the odd large fish up to 3 kg. Dry flies and nymphs should succeed. I clearly remember, as a 10-year-old, watching the skills of two 15-year-old country girls tickling trout in the Hawkins River behind Racecourse Hill. They were very successful, though their enthusiasm was somewhat tempered when one of them tickled a large eel by mistake.

L11, Irwell River and Harts Creek

Location and access   These streams all enter Lake Ellesmere –
the L11 at Selwyn Huts, the Irwell near Irwell and Doyleston, and
Harts Creek further south near Lakeside. Lake Road crosses the
Irwell near the mouth, while the Leeston–Christchurch road crosses
at Heslops Corner. Harts Creek can be reached from Leeston and
Lake and Harts roads south of Leeston.

All these streams flow across farmland and hold small brown trout
in their middle reaches. However, the rather sluggish, willow-lined
lower reaches promise good runs of larger estuarine-living browns from
Lake Ellesmere, especially after dark and early in the season, when
fish come upstream chasing smelt. Try Hart Creek, Red Shadow, Hairy
Dog, Fuzzy Wuzzy and Hope's Dark. Again, recent droughts and
increasing eutrophication in Lake Ellesmere has caused a deterioration
in the fishing.

Rakaia River

Location   Rises in the Southern Alps west of Lake Coleridge and
flows east across the Canterbury Plains to enter the Pacific Ocean
south of Lake Ellesmere.

Access   This is not difficult, though adjacent roads often run along
high river terraces some distance from the river. The Rakaia Huts
at the mouth can be reached from Southbridge, S.H.1 crosses the
river at Rakaia, the Rakaia–Highbank road follows up the true
right bank, while S.H.72 crosses the river inland at Rakaia Gorge.
From Rakaia Gorge, roads follow the river upstream on both sides.
Despite this, access is much easier by jet boat and many salmon
anglers use this method of transport.

Season   1 October–30 April. Winter extension below S.H.1 from
first Saturday following Queen's Birthday Weekend to 31 August.
Closed season from 1 March to 30 April above Lake Coleridge
powerhouse and in the tailrace of the Highbank power station from
1 October to 30 September.

This large, snow-fed river with an unstable shingle bed is, like its
counterpart the Waimakariri, prone to flooding and changes of course.

It is not recommended as a trout fishery as the water often contains glacial silt, though an occasional good sea-run brown is caught, usually by salmon anglers. It has a high reputation as a salmon river, and few anglers fish this river exclusively for trout. Some trout are landed, however, mostly by local anglers fishing in the vicinity of the Great Island below S.H.1 and at the back of the Rakaia golf course. As the river is prone to changing course from season to season, local knowledge is essential.

South Canterbury District

This diverse district contains lively small-stream brown trout fishing in the farming country near Ashburton and Temuka, a number of hydro lakes on the severely modified Waitaki River, and some contrasting high-country rivers, lakes and tarns. In addition, the large snow-fed Rangitata and Waitaki rivers are highly regarded as salmon fisheries.

Unless otherwise stated, the season opens on 1 October and closes on 30 April. The bag limit in the South Canterbury district is 14 trout or salmon — the limit for salmon is 4, the limit for trout 10. In the high-country lakes the bag limit is 6 trout or salmon, of which not more than 4 may be salmon. No more than 5 trout may be taken from Deep Stream (which flows into Lake Aviemore), the Otematata or the Maerewhenua rivers. Minimum size is 35 cm in Lakes Alexandrina and McGregor and 25 cm elsewhere.

Ashburton River

Location   Rises in the Arrowsmith Range of the Southern Alps, flows east through a gorge, then across the plains to pass just south of Ashburton and enter the sea south-east of the town.

Access   There are good roads running almost to the headwaters. S.H.1 crosses at Ashburton while S.H.72 crosses at Mt Somers. Access is easier from roads following the true left bank or north side of the river. Many side roads off the Ashburton–Staveley road running parallel to, but south of, S.H.77 lead to the river. The Ashburton Gorge road from Mt Somers leads to the upper reaches.

Season   A winter extension applies below the S.H.1 bridge from the first Saturday following Queen's Birthday Weekend to 31 August. Elsewhere, 1 October–31 March. The river is closed during April to allow salmon to spawn.

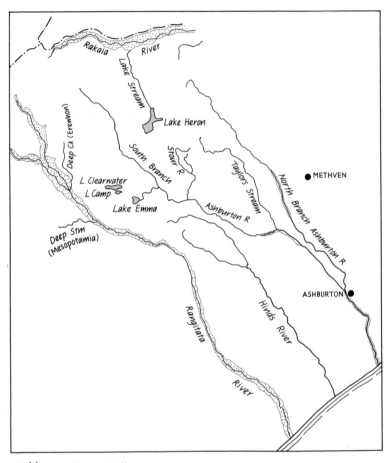

Ashburton River Valley

There are north and south branches which joint west of Ashburton, but only the south branch is worth fishing. The waters of the north branch often dry up in summer and disappear beneath the shingle. Efforts by the Catchment Board to straighten the river have not helped this fishery.

There is reasonable stream fishing for small brown trout in clear water from below Ashburton to above the Ashburton Gorge at Hakatere Junction, providing there is plenty of water. The river runs over a shingle bed and is safe to cross and wade. The banks are lined with willows (especially below S.H.1), gorse, broom and scrub.

Trout average 0.5–1 kg and on bright clear days can be spotted in pools and shallow runs. Flows tend to diminish in summer when water is removed for irrigation and in these conditions a very careful approach is required. Use small nymphs and dry flies in sizes 14–18. I have had success with flies as small as a size 20 Red Spinner tied without wings. A good evening rise occurs beneath the willows in warm conditions. Try a small wet fly such as Twilight Beauty or Hardy's Favourite. Salmon run in this river from February to April providing there is a good flow rate.

Hinds River

> **Location and access** Rises in the Moorhouse Range and runs parallel to, but some 20 km south of, the Ashburton River. S.H.1 crosses the river just north of Hinds while S.H.72 crosses inland at Mayfield. There are plenty of side roads offering easy access.
>
> **Restrictions** Fly fishing only.

A similar river to the Ashburton but much smaller and rain-fed, the Hinds can be clear and fishable when the snow-fed Ashburton River is silt-laden and unfishable. However, some stretches can dry and even disappear entirely beneath the shingle in long, hot summers. It holds a limited stock of small brown trout. Use a long trace of 1–2 kg nylon, a weight-forward No. 4–6 floating line and size 16–20 dry flies and nymphs. May the nor'wester not blow!

Lake Heron and other lakes close by

These are all exposed high-country lakes subject to the vagaries of north-west storms. Snow can fall at any time of the year except during February. The season runs from the first Saturday in November to 30 April, except at Lake Camp where the season extends to 31 May. (See map for locations.)

Lake Heron

> **Location** Lies between the headwaters of the Rakaia and Ashburton rivers south-west of Methven.
>
> **Access** From Mt Somers take the Ashburton Gorge road to

Hakatere Junction. Branch to the right for Lakes Heron and Emily and the Maori Lakes, but branch to the left for Lakes Emma, Roundabout, Spider, Donne, Camp and Clearwater.

Restrictions   The bag limit is 4 trout or 8 salmon, but the season closes for salmon on the last day in February. Fishing is permitted from an anchored boat provided it is not mechanically powered, and artificial minnow and natural bait are allowed.

Lake Heron contains good-condition brown and rainbow trout in the 1.5–2.3 kg range that can be spotted cruising the lake shore. In addition, large quinnat salmon enter the lake from the Rakaia River and spawn in Mellish Stream, flowing into the lake on the eastern shore. The shores are tussock-covered with a few patches of willow. Fish will accept all types of flies, including Muddler Minnow and Rabbit pattern lures, Coch-y-bondhu, Royal Wulff, Dad's Favourite and Black Gnat dry flies, and Pheasant Tail and Dragon Fly nymphs fished on a floating line to cruising trout. Spinning is also productive.

As a 15-year-old I camped here with my parents and, much to their astonishment, landed a 7.8 kg quinnat salmon on a small spinning rod. The fish took me an hour to land and was in excellent condition despite its long journey up the Rakaia River and into the lake. Many years ago, the Lake Station owners, when short of fish, would walk the lake shores on windy days armed with a pitchfork. Cruising trout would actually get washed ashore while searching for food along the lake edge, and then swim back on the next wave, providing of course they escaped the pitchfork.

There are basic camping facilities under the basket willows near where the road first reaches the lake.

The Lake Stream draining the northern end of Lake Heron joins the Cameron River before entering the Rakaia. From the outlet the upper reaches of this stream flow over a shingle bed lined by willows. The middle reaches are swampy and difficult; the lower reaches become quite boisterous. The surrounding tussock-covered hills and occasional patch of beech bush greatly enhances the scenic beauty here, but the nor'wester can rapidly drive a fly angler to drink! Even on calm, bright mornings, the wind tends to get up around 10 a.m. Fish can be spotted and taken on dry flies and sunk nymphs or black lures fished after dark, but stocks are not high.

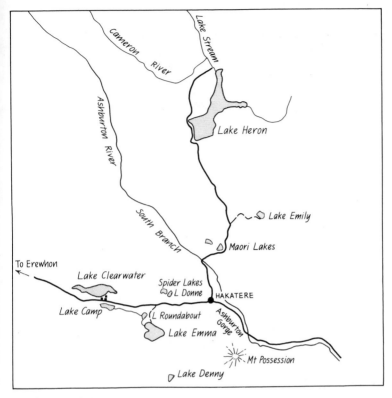

Ashburton lakes

Lake Emily

Access   About 3 km along the road from the Maori Lakes to Lake Heron there is a gate and a signpost on the right where the road turns left. A 3 km tramp leads to this lake along an old track that winds up a hill. A locked gate prevents vehicular access.

Restrictions   Fly fishing only.

This small, exposed lake lies in a barren tussock basin. There are no willows to impede the backcast, but the nor'wester is a problem. The lake contains fontinalis, or American brook trout, and brown and rainbow trout, but spotting is not easy.

Maori Lakes

These two small lakes are passed on the road to Lake Heron. There is limited shoreline access as the lake margins are very swampy, and the best fishing is from a small boat or float tube. Nevertheless these lakes contain large brown trout, especially in the lake furthest from the road. The fish dive for the weed beds when hooked.

Note: Fly fishing only.

Lake Emma

Access   Signposted on the Clearwater road about 4.5 km from the Hakatere Junction. A track leads from a gate to the lake about 1.5 km away. You can drive in during fine weather but a four-wheel-drive is advisable.

Lake Emma holds browns and rainbows, which are best fished with a spinner or lure of the bully type on a slow-sinking line, such as Hamill's Killer, Mrs Simpson or Muddler Minnow. However, in clear conditions cruising fish can be spotted and stalked with a dry fly or cicada imitation, especially along the swampy western shore. Water clarity has not been improved by the high swan population.

Lake Roundabout

This small lake can be seen on the right from the track to Lake Emma. It contains only brown trout, which will respond to similar methods as for Lake Emma. Niggerheads and a red weed pose some problems.

Note: Fly fishing only.

Lake Camp

This lake lies on the opposite side of the road to Lake Clearwater, and contains brown and rainbow trout that respond to spinning, lures of the bully type and dry flies early or late in the day, but the lake is often disturbed by powerboats and water-skiers in summer. An extended season − to 31 May − applies.

Lake Clearwater

This lake, the largest along the Clearwater road, lies on the right side of the road driving in, opposite Lake Camp. There is a fishing village on the shoreline, which is surrounded by tussock and a few willows. It contains only browns in the 1–1.5 kg range. There's good fishing at the stream outlet at the eastern end of the lake and cruising fish can be stalked along the shoreline in bright, calm conditions. Dabchicks nest close to the village. Basic camping facilities are available.

Lakes Denny, Spider and Donne

These lakes hold brown trout and are limited to fly fishing only. There's a four-wheel-drive track from Hakatere Junction to Lake Denny. The access track to Donne and Spider lakes is signposted and lies almost opposite the track to Lake Emma. It's a 45-minute walk to the lakes, which lie in barren, exposed tussock basins.

I prefer fishing all these high-country lakes in calm, clear, bright conditions. The prevailing nor'wester often ruins promising days. Fish must be carefully stalked and cast to well in front of their cruising beat; they are easily frightened if you cast at them. It pays to have a friend spotting for you. A slow-sinking or sink tip line is an advantage as a floating line, even the trace, will cast a shadow in bright, sunny conditions. Heavily weighted nymphs will sink too far and get caught in the weed, so I use a lightly weighted nymph or small wet fly. Fish can still be seen even when a good ripple disturbs the surface, but care must be taken and polaroids are essential for spotting. Dry flies are readily accepted when a ripple disturbs the shadow and blurs the reflection. The disadvantage with blind fishing is that large stretches of dead water, with no fish in the vicinity, may be covered.

Rangitata River

Location and access   Rises in the Southern Alps and after emerging from a gorge flows east in braided fashion across the Canterbury Plains to enter the sea south of Hinds. Many roads give access to this large river, though salmon anglers often find a jet boat the most convenient means of access.

Season   This large snow-fed river is mainly used by anglers for salmon fishing and restrictions apply because of this. Below S.H.1 there is a winter extension from the first Saturday following Queen's Birthday Weekend to 31 August; and in the Rangitata Diversion Race from 1 May to 30 September. There's a closed season from 1 March to 30 April above Red Rocks Bluff and from the west end of the Rangitata Gorge downstream to the confluence with Boundary Creek. Elsewhere, 1 October–30 April.

Like its northern neighbour the Rakaia, the Rangitata River is a highly regarded salmon fishery, although some large trout are also caught, usually by salmon anglers on spinners. Very few anglers fish exclusively for trout. The river is unstable, braided and often silt-laden. Between the lower end of the gorge and S.H.1 trout stocks are not high.

Above the Rangitata Gorge there are some relatively inaccessible side creeks that contain both brown and rainbow trout.

Deep Stream, on Mesopotamia Station south of the Rangitata, and Deep Creek, on Erewhon Station north of the river, are two such streams. Good-sized fish can be caught on spinners or sunk lures. Salmon also spawn in these streams, so in January and February you are never quite sure just what type of fish has taken your lure. An occasional good-sized brown trout can be caught from the stretch of river behind Peel Forest.

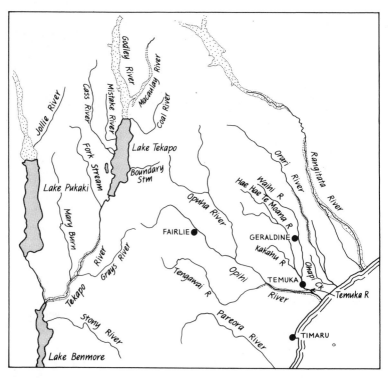

South Canterbury rivers

Orari River

Location   Rises from the Ben McLeod Range, flows on a south-easterly course parallel to, but south of, the Rangitata River and enters the sea north of Temuka.

Access   Surrounded by a maze of roads, with S.H.1 crossing at Orari and S.H.72 crossing inland north of Geraldine at Orari Bridge.

Similar in character but larger than the Hinds River, the Orari is popular with anglers but does not hold large stocks of fish. Brown and rainbow trout can be caught in the 0.5–1 kg range, with quinnat salmon spawning in the river late in the season, providing there is sufficient water flow and the mouth is open, which has not been the case recently. It has a shingle bed and is willow-lined, with reduced water flows in hot summers, so it is best fished early in the season. The gorge holds small numbers of small brown trout (25 fish/km). Use very small dry flies and nymphs on fine gear.

Ohapi Creek

Location and access   This small, clear, spring-fed tributary of the Orari flows parallel to, but south of, the lower reaches of the Orari. Access is difficult and mainly across private farmland and north-east of Temuka and just north of Milford School.

Restrictions   Fly fishing only.

This stream, highly regarded by the dry fly purist, holds average stocks of brown trout in the 0.5–1 kg range. The stream is narrow with grassy and willow-lined banks. Wading is unnecessary and disturbs fish. Use very small caddis and mayfly imitations on a fine tippet.

Opihi River and tributaries

Opihi River

Location and access   Drains the Ben McLeod and Richmond ranges west of Fairlie and follows an easterly course to enter the sea east of Temuka. Good access just south of Temuka from S.H.1 from Pleasant Point, Opihi, Raincliff and Fairlie.

The willow-lined Opihi holds brown trout in the 0.5–1.5 kg range with a small run of salmon in February–April providing the shingle bar at the mouth is open, but it can dry in summer, with water disappearing beneath the shingle, and suffers from eutrophication, so it's best fished early in the season. Stocks are reasonable near the S.H.1 bridge (30 fish/km), but the fish are mainly small at Rockwood Bridge (15 fish/km). Catchment Board activities have not helped this river, though it is still reasonably popular with local anglers.

Opuha River

Location and access   Joins the Opihi River at Raincliff just south of Opuha. Crossed by S.H.79 just north of this confluence. Good access off Gudex Road.

This small stream running over a gravel bed holds small brown trout. It is pleasant dry fly water though fish stocks are not great and flows are often much reduced in summer.

Hae Hae Te Moana River

Location and access   Rises west of Geraldine and joins the Opihi near Temuka. Crossed by S.H.79 just south-west of Geraldine. Access also from side roads off Earl Road.

This small, shingly, willow-lined stream holds small brown trout and is best fished early in the season before the water warms. There is reasonable water near Geraldine. A small tributary, the Kakahu, holds small browns – access at Hilton.

Waihi River

Location and access   Rises from the Four Peak Range, flows through the Waihi Gorge to Geraldine, then turns south to join the Hae Hae Te Moana River. S.H.72 follows the river from Geraldine to Winchester.

The Waihi has reasonable stocks of small brown trout and there's some good fly water, especially in the middle reaches. It is best fished early in the season.

Nymphing the Temuka — a highly recommended fly river.

Temuka River

Location and access Formed by the confluence of the Hae Hae Te Moana and Waihi rivers just north-west of Temuka. Flows west and south of Temuka before joining the lower reaches of the Opihi. Crossed by the Waitohi–Temuka road at Manse Bridge and S.H.1.

The Temuka holds browns in the 0.5–1.3 kg range. Because water flows are reasonably consistent even in summer, this is the best stream in the Temuka district. There are attractive pools and riffles, the river is easy to wade and cross, and fish stocks are good. There's excellent water below the S.H.1 bridge, and an active evening rise occurs on summer evenings. It has grassy and willow-lined banks and a shingle bed, and fish are easy to spot but scare easily during bright daytime conditions. Try small dry flies such as Red Quill Gnat, Twilight Beauty, Blue Dun and Coch-y-bondhu in sizes 16–18 or lightly weighted nymphs in similar sizes, such as Caddis, Pheasant Tail and Red Tipped Governor. A small wet fly fished across and down on a floating line will also take fish in the evenings. This river is highly recommended to the dry fly angler.

Tengawai River

Location and access   Drains the Richmond Range and follows S.H.8 from Albury to Pleasant Point, where it joins the Opihi.

Restrictions   Fly fishing only.

This is another small, shingly, willow-lined river holding small brown trout, which respond to mayfly imitations such as Red Quill Gnat or Dad's Favourite dry flies in the smaller sizes. During the evening rise, try a small Twilight Beauty wet fly on a floating line. Like all the Temuka streams it is best early in the season before water flows reduce and weed growth becomes a problem.

All these small South Canterbury rivers were once highly regarded and delightful brown trout habitats before farming operations and catchment activities reduced water flows, disturbed riverbeds and induced eutrophication and weed growth in summer. Some stretches now dry completely.

The Paeroa River south of Timaru has been ruined by water draw-off for irrigation. It was once a popular stream and still yields some trout to local anglers, mainly from the gorge area early in the season.

The Waihao River, located 5 km south of Waimate, holds small browns, and most anglers use live bait to catch these in the lower reaches, especially after a fresh.

Kakanui River

Location and access   Rises in the Kakanui Mountains west of Oamaru and follows a south-westerly course to enter the sea south of Oamaru at Kakanui. S.H.1 crosses just north of Maheno, and a number of roads both upstream and downstream of this bridge offer access to the river, often across private farmland.

The best water lies below Clifton Falls where there are good stable holding pools and shallow, shingly runs. The banks are willow-lined and fish are easily spotted in clear water. The Kakanui holds browns in the 0.5–1.3 kg range but is not heavily fished. Drift dives near S.H.1 north of Maheno have revealed surprisingly high numbers of small and medium-sized brown trout (80 fish/km at Pringles). There are good estuarine or sea-run browns at the mouth, especially early in the season after a fresh when the whitebait are running. There are few fish above Clifton Falls. This is an excellent small stream for the fly angler.

The Waianakarua River, crossed by S.H.1 south of Herbert, also holds a few browns, but the river warms and becomes low and weedy in summer.

Lower Waitaki River

Location Rises in the Southern Alps, drains three large high-country lakes and flows on an easterly course to enter the sea at Glenavy, north of Oamaru.

Access
The mouth from Glenavy.
Lower reaches (below Lake Waitaki) S.H.83 follows the true right bank from Georgetown to Lake Waitaki. S.H.82 follows the true left bank from Ikawai to Kurow. Branch roads off S.H.83, such as Wilson's, Goulding and Jardine roads, lead to the south bank of the river. From S.H.82 there is access at Hentridges, Ferry Road and the Stone Wall. A jet boat is useful in this area as there are thousands of islands and braided streams, some difficult to cross. In many places access is through private land, and the river is often some distance from the road.
Upper reaches The upper reaches have been converted into hydro lakes and will be dealt with separately.

Restrictions No salmon fishing is permitted above Bortons in April.

This is a large river, though it has been severely modified for hydro-electric power generation and water flows are not always consistent – anglers beware of sudden fluctuations! It flows over an unstable shingle bed and the banks are generally willowed. Some stretches can only be reached by boat as the river follows a braided course below Lake Waitaki. The water is sometimes a milky green colour owing to glacial silt, but in summer clarity is usually good.

There are good-sized brown and rainbow trout here, most of which are caught by spinning. There's often a good sedge rise late in the evenings, especially just below the Hakataramea confluence. Good water can be reached from an access track down the true left bank below the Kurow Bridge.

A few good sea-run fish are taken by salmon anglers at the mouth on spinners. This is a famous quinnat salmon river, the first salmon having been introduced from the Hakataramea Hatchery in 1901. The Demonstration Channels at Duntroon hold good stocks of fish, but a special permit, obtainable on site, is required to fish these channels.

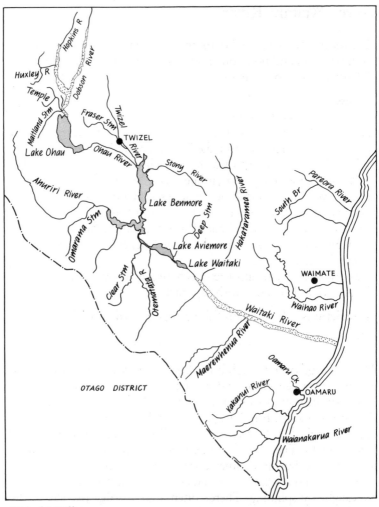

Waitaki Valley

Maerewhenua River

Location and access   Rises near Danseys Pass in the Kakanui Mountains and flows north to join the Waitaki at Duntroon. Road to Livingstone and Danseys Pass follows up the river.

Restrictions   Fly fishing only; no salmon fishing. The bag limit is 5 fish.

Once the Maerewhenua was a highly regarded river, before water was extracted for irrigation. The lower reaches are shingly and hold both brown and rainbows, but stocks are not plentiful. Fish can be spotted but tend to be shy in bright summer conditions and a careful approach with small dry flies or nymphs is essential for success. There's reasonable fishing in the vicinity of Kelly's Gully (15 fish/km), but the fish tend to be small. The best fishing is early in the season. The upper reaches provide more stable water and a few deep pools in gorgy tussock country, which hold a few good browns providing you do not mind walking.

The beautiful Horseshoe Tarn in the Ahuriri Valley.

Hakataramea River

Location   Rises in the Mackenzie Country south of Fairlie and flows on a southerly course to join the Waitaki River at Hakataramea on the opposite bank to Kurow.

Access   Hakataramea Valley and McHenrys roads follow up both sides of the river from Hakataramea.

Restrictions   Fly fishing only.

This favoured salmon spawning stream was subjected to severe flooding in 1985 followed by a drought. It holds good stocks (140 fish/km) of small brown and rainbow which can be spotted and fished for with dry flies or nymphs. Early in the season there is 30 km of fishable water, but fish tend to drop back downstream during low-water summer conditions. A very popular small stream with easy access, it has a shingle bed and is fringed with willows.

Lake Waitaki

Location   This is the first hydro lake just upstream from Kurow.

Access   From S.H.83. There's a boat ramp below Aviemore Dam on the northern side.

Season   1 October–30 April.

Restrictions   Fishing is prohibited in the river adjacent to the spawning race below Lake Aviemore.

Waitaki holds brown and rainbow averaging 1 kg generally fished for by deep trolling from a boat or live bait fishing. The lake water is sometimes milky from glacial sediment. There are some shallow inlets adjacent to the main road where fish can be spotted and stalked in bright conditions. There's a basic campsite at Fisherman's Bend.

Lake Aviemore

Location   This is the central lake of three on the Waitaki River.

Access   Is encircled by roads, including Te Akatarawa Road.

Season   Open all year except September.

This 16 km-long lake holds good stocks of brown and rainbow averaging 0.75–1.5 kg. Most fish are taken by spinning from the shore or trolling from a boat. There are a few fly fishing spots, especially along the shallow shoreline adjacent to the main road (S.H.83), where

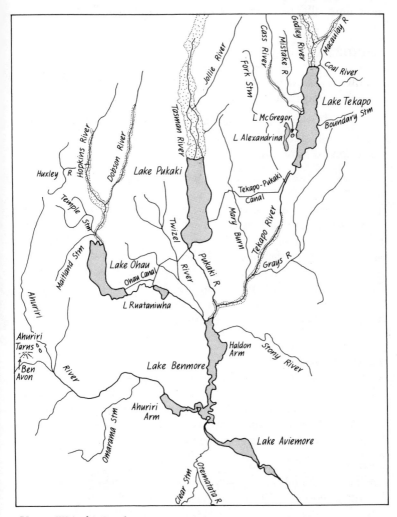

Upper Waitaki Catchment

fish can be taken by all fly methods. Other useful spots are the Otematata River delta, the lower reaches of this stream and some of the small stream mouths, where cruising fish can be seen on their beat.

The deep water above the Aviemore Dam and at the mouth of Deep Stream is worth fishing at night with a well-sunk night lure, either from the shore or from a boat. Wind is the main problem in the Waitaki Valley: the nor'wester blows down the valley and the sou'wester blows up. Wind from any other direction is welcome but most unusual! There are basic camping facilities at Waitangi.

Otematata River

Location   Rises in the Hawkdun and Ida ranges of Central Otago and flows north to enter Lake Aviemore at Otematata.

Access   Permission must be obtained from Otematata Station for access to the middle and upper reaches. A four-wheel-drive vehicle is a decided advantage.

Season   First Saturday in November–30 April.

This excellent medium-sized, stable river has well-developed pools and runs flowing through isolated, barren, hilly tussock country. It holds browns and rainbows up to 2 kg and fish can be spotted. The Clear Stream tributary offers another 10 km of excellent water, but a great deal of tramping is required to fish this stretch of river. Use weighted Hare and Copper, Pheasant Tail and Half Back nymphs or Dad's Favourite, Deer Hair Bivisible and Coch-y-bondhu dry flies in sizes 12–16. Catch and release is recommended.

Lake Benmore

Location   Lies in the Mackenzie Country between Twizel, Omarama and Otematata. Boat ramps are located at Sailors Cutting on Ahuriri Arm and off Grays Road at the Haldon Boat Harbour. There are also excellent camping facilities at both these locations.

Access
- Turn off S.H.8 at Dog Kennel Corner near Burke Pass and take the Haldon road to the east side of Haldon Arm.
- The Tekapo Canal road (leaves S.H.8 opposite the road to Lake

Alexandrina) and its extension, the Ministry of Works Tekapo–Pukaki River road, follow the true right bank of the Tekapo River from the Tekapo powerhouse to Haldon Arm. This is a dry-weather road as there are unbridged fords. There is a bridge across the lower Tekapo River.

- From Ruataniwha Dam a road leads to the west side of Haldon Arm.
- From S.H.83, take the road to the Benmore Dam and Ahuriri delta.

Season   Like Lake Aviemore this lake is open all year round except for the month of September.

Restrictions   The bag limit is 10 fish.

Formed in 1964, this large lake has 116 km of rather inaccessible shoreline. There are two arms to the lake: Haldon Arm with its somewhat milky glacial water from the Tasman Glacier and from spillway discharges; and Ahuriri Arm with clear snow-fed river water. The lake holds vast stocks of brown and rainbow trout and landlocked sockeye salmon.

Most fish are taken by deep trolling from boats using lead lines, or live-bait fishing with worms, but cruising fish can be spotted in the shallower bays in favourable summer conditions, especially when the lake is not too high. The Black Forest area on the eastern shoreline is a favoured spot. Trout average 0.75–1.5 kg.

The Ahuriri mouth and delta is very popular for fly fishing, especially at night with a sunk black lure such as Hairy Dog, Black Phantom, Mrs Simpson or Fuzzy Wuzzy. During the day cruising fish can be stalked and cast to in the shallows, along the edges of the tussock shore and over the weed beds with a small, lightly weighted nymph, wet fly or dry fly of the Coch-y-bondhu, Royal Wulff or Palmer varieties. However, keep low and out of sight of cruising fish as they tend to be very wary. The lake level will often determine the catch rate in this area. If it is flat calm, then cast onto a sandy patch and activate the fly when a fish approaches. Casting at fish in these clear conditions will only scare them off.

Winter fishing is quite popular in this lake and good catches are made deep trolling from boats even when the surrounding countryside is covered with snow. Survival gear should be worn during these conditions!

Stony River

Location and access Flows into the Haldon Arm of Lake Benmore near Haldon. Use a boat for the lower reaches. Permission should be obtained from Haldon Station before tramping across private farmland for the middle and upper reaches.

This rock and stone river, which holds a few browns and rainbows in the 1–2 kg range, is quite highly regarded although access is not easy and the river tends to dry in hot summers. During such conditions, there are a few cold stable gorge pools well upstream. Fish can be taken on flies or spinners.

Omarama River

Location Drains the foot of the St Bathans Range south of Omarama and flows north to join the Ahuriri River at Omarama just above Lake Benmore. It flows through the Omarama camping ground.

Access Take the road from Omarama to the Tara Hills Research Station. This follows up the true left bank.

The fine trout waters of the Ahuriri River winding through Ben Avon Station.

The Omarama holds browns averaging 1–2 kg, usually in good condition, with a few up to 4 kg in peat-stained water. They are very difficult to spot and should be fished for blind with a sunk Pheasant Tail, Half Back or Caddis nymph; they are even more difficult to land, being adept at tangling round willow roots. There's fishing all the way to well above the Tara Hills bridge. The lower reaches tend to be willow-choked and hold smaller fish.

Ahuriri River

Location   Rises in the Southern Alps below Mt Huxley and between Lakes Ohau and Hawea. Flows on a curving easterly course to enter Lake Benmore near Omarama.

Access   The delta has been described under Lake Benmore. Although some distance away, S.H.8 runs parallel to the river from Omarama to Dunstan Downs Station; it then turns south towards Lindis Pass. The shingle road to Birchwood and Ben Avon stations follows the river upstream for 25 km from this point. It is a relatively short walk across to the river from this road, but permission should be obtained from the stations before crossing private land to fish.

Season   First Saturday in November–30 April. Above Longslip Creek and in the east branch, first Saturday in December–30 April.

Restrictions   The bag limit below Longslip Creek is 5 fish; above Longslip and in the east branch, 3 fish. No live-bait fishing in this river.

This medium-sized river has a high reputation, and deservedly so. The middle and lower reaches are willow-lined, braided, shingly and unstable, and flow across exposed tussock and lupin flats but still hold good stocks of brown and rainbow in the 1–1.5 kg range (90 fish/km), especially in the stretch from the S.H.8 bridge to the lake. Most fish are taken from this area on spinners or lures fished across and down, but there's also excellent nymph fishing. Downstream lure fishing tends to attract smaller fish and these should be carefully returned.

There's good water where fish can be spotted higher upstream in the vicinity of Ben Avon Station where the river follows a convoluted course (please ask permission here). The backwaters often hold good fish, but one must be prepared to cast to fish facing downstream – a tricky prospect because of drag. The upper reaches above Birchwood

Station hold only a few fish (2 fish/km on drift dives), up to 4.5 kg in clear pools and runs. These are mainly cunning browns with x-ray vision which pose a real challenge. The nor'wester whistles down this valley so make the most of an upstream breeze! By 10 a.m. the wind invariably blows down the valley. Wading is not difficult and the river can be crossed between pools in selected places but is best fished in boots and shorts.

Suggested flies include Dad's Favourite, Coch-y-bondhu, Kakahi Queen and Deer Hair dry flies, Hare and Copper, Perla, Half Back and Pheasant Tail weighted nymphs, and lures such as Rabbit varieties, Lord's Killer, Yellow Dorothy or Mrs Simpson. The mountain views looking upstream compensate to some extent for the prevailing wind. The riverbed provides one of the last habitats for the endangered black stilt.

Ben Avon and Horseshoe Tarns (Ahuriri Valley Tarns)

> **Location and access**   These lagoons are accessible off the Ben Avon road on private land 2 km north of Ben Avon Station. The lagoons lie between the road and the Ahuriri River.
>
> **Season**   First Saturday in December–30 April.
>
> **Restrictions**   Fly fishing only.

These waters contain large browns which cruise in tantalising fashion off weed beds. They don't seem interested in dry flies but will take a nymph provided you can keep it out of the weeds. Use a size 14–18 non-weighted nymph or a sparsely tied small wet fly on a long greased cast and if you hook a fish and land it you can be well satisfied. I spent hours on one cruising fish without success but enjoyed myself thoroughly.

Like most lake-living browns these fish have a regular beat and are so predictable they can be timed. Woe betide any fish that stray onto foreign territory – they are quickly chased away by the occupier! The shore is swampy with a few willows. When the Ahuriri River floods, these lagoons can also become lightly silt-laden. The lagoon lying on the left-hand side of the road just before the turn-off to Ben Avon also holds a few large browns.

Lake Ohau

Location   Lies south-west of Twizel between the Ben Ohau and Barrier ranges.

Access   Branch off S.H.8 at Clearburn on the Lake Ohau Lodge road for the southern shore and head of the lake. The road to Glen Lyon Station from Twizel skirts the northern shore. There are boat-launching ramps 3 km beyond the Lodge turn-off and at the control gates.

Season   First Saturday in November–30 April.

Restrictions   Trolling is not permitted within 200 m of a shore angler, the mouth of the Dobson River or the outlet. The bag limit is 10 fish.

Ohau is a 16 km-long deep blue picturesque high-country lake often swept by nor'westers from the Dobson and Hopkins valleys. It can become silt-laden for a week at a time when the Dobson and Hopkins rivers are in flood. The lake holds good stocks of 1–2 kg browns and rainbow, though I saw a beautiful 4 kg rainbow landed on a Mrs Simpson lure at the mouth of Parson's Creek late one evening. There are also some resident sockeye salmon.

The lake is good for spinning and trolling, but fly fishing is restricted to stream mouths at night and the shallows between Lake Ohau Lodge and the head of the lake. Here the shoreline consists of tussock, manuka and matagouri scrub and this can impede the backcast, especially when the lake is high. Cruising fish can be spotted over weed beds and cast to in this area. Wading can be treacherous at the Dobson Delta because of soft shingle and sand brought down by the river, so fishing is best from a boat. The lake tends to be under-fished.

Lake Middleton

Location   Lies adjacent to Lake Ohau, where an attractive camping ground is sited.

Season   First Saturday in November–30 April.

This lake contains small brown and rainbow trout, but the lake is often disturbed by water-skiers and swimmers, and there's better fishing in streams close by.

Maitland Stream

> **Location and access**   Drains the Barrier Range and follows a north-easterly course to join the Dobson River at the head of Lake Ohau. The Ohau road crosses this stream at the head of the lake.
>
> **Season**   First Saturday in November–30 April.

Maitland holds a few browns and rainbows in clear, fast mountain water. In the lower reaches, it is unstable and there are few fish below the roadbridge. This stream is best fished early in the season by tackling the rough gorge 0.5 km upstream above the bridge. There are a few good resident fish in the gorge that will accept dry flies and well-weighted nymphs. You are unlikely to be disturbed as the going is not easy.

Temple Stream

> **Location and access**   The north and south branches drain the Barrier Range north-west of Lake Ohau and meet near the road end at the Temple Forest picnic and camping ground. The river then follows a southerly course, leaves the bush and meanders in a braided fashion across farmland to join the lower reaches of the Dobson River. The Ohau road crosses Temple Stream 5 km beyond the Maitland crossing with a branch road leading to the forks at the Temple Forest picnic ground.
>
> **Season**   First Saturday in November–30 April.

This fast-flowing mountain torrent holds few fish above the forks. There are one or two pools worth exploring in a gorge 2 km downstream from the picnic ground, but the best water lies in the lower 2 km where the river crosses farmland. In parts the stream is infested with willows, but an occasional good fish can be spotted, especially early in the season.

There are a few large fish in the deeper holes of the lower reaches of the Hopkins and Dobson rivers, but these are unstable, shingly, snow-fed rivers prone to flooding and course changes. Dust storms can make life unpleasant in this area. The tramper/angler should look at the Huxley flowing into the Hopkins. It is gorgy and difficult but holds a few large trout — just the sort of river to find a trophy fish.

The once highly regarded Ohau River was destroyed by hydro development in 1980 and 'replaced' by Lake Ruataniwha, which has been stocked with rainbow trout. The nearby Wairepo Lake contains mainly browns and both lakes are best fished with spinning gear or by trolling behind a boat. These lakes are easily viewed from S.H.8 between Twizel and Omarama.

Grays River

Location and access   Drains swampy country near Burke Pass, flows south and joins the Tekapo River. Haldon Road turns off S.H.8 at Dog Kennel Corner, west off Burke Pass, to the Haldon Arm of Lake Benmore and follows the true left bank for some distance. There are rough four-wheel-drive tracks across private farmland to the river off this road. The Ministry of Works Tekapo–Pukaki road, an extension of the Tekapo Canal road, runs down the true right bank of the Tekapo River to the confluence with Grays River and the Mary Burn. Four-wheel-drive vehicles are advised for this road as there are some fords which, though negotiable in dry weather, become difficult after rain. A rough metalled track follows up the true left bank of the Tekapo River to the Grays River confluence.
Season   First Saturday in November–30 April.

This river holds good-sized brown and rainbow trout in a succession of clear pools and runs. There's 5–6 km of fishable water upstream from the Tekapo confluence. The river has a shingly bed and grassy and willow-lined banks, and is best fished in December–January in the middle and lower reaches where there is excellent fly water, though it does tend to dry over a long, hot summer.

Tekapo River

Location   Drains Lake Tekapo and flows south to enter Haldon Arm on Lake Benmore. The Tekapo–Pukaki Canal road leaves S.H.8 opposite the Glenmore–Godley Peaks road and follows down the true right bank finally crossing the lower reaches above Haldon Arm. A rough metalled road follows up the true left bank from Haldon Arm to the Grays River confluence.

The upper reaches are virtually dry as a result of hydro-electric power modification. The river only becomes worthwhile below the Forks Stream confluence and is fishable only below the Mary Burn confluence in the Grays Hills area. However, the river holds remarkably high numbers of good-sized browns and rainbows (250 fish/km on drift dives) despite fluctuating water flows. It has a shingle bed, is willow-lined in parts and flows through barren rabbit-infested tussock country. Most fish are taken on spinning gear though there is also good fly fishing. The river, which has some very deep holes, easily becomes unfishable after rain mainly owing to silt brought down by the Forks Stream. Landlocked sockeye salmon from Lake Benmore spawn in this river.

Lake Pukaki

Even though the lake level has been raised and the water is constantly discoloured by glacial silt, a few good fish are caught at stream mouths. Try a Hamill's Killer lure or even a dry fly at the mouth of Lagoon Creek on a calm evening and you may be pleasantly surprised. The season is open all year here.

The Tekapo–Pukaki hydro canal, crossed by S.H.8 between these two lakes, the Pukaki–Ohau hydro canal behind Twizel and the Ohau Canal all hold fish and are open all year round. Roads generally follow the canal banks. Aesthetically the canals may leave a little to be desired, but a good number of fish are taken from these waters, usually on spinning gear, though fish can be spotted along the edges feeding on insects drifting into the water from the tussock banks. Most are rainbow in the 1–2 kg range but provide good sport. Some enterprising local anglers patrol the canals on motorbikes, stopping when they spot a fish.

Twizel River

Location and access   Drains the Ben Ohau Range, flows on a southerly course through the outskirts of Twizel township and eventually enters the Haldon Arm of Lake Benmore. Crossed by S.H.8 near Twizel.

This river has a shingle bed and is willow-lined in parts with well-developed pools and runs. It holds a good stock of brown trout that can be spotted in clear conditions. Effluent from Twizel township was thought to have polluted this river, but I found it pleasant and worthwhile to fish, especially downstream from S.H.8.

Mary Burn

Location and access   Flows on a southerly course parallel to the eastern shoreline of Lake Pukaki, is crossed by S.H.8, and eventually joins the Tekapo River in the Grays Hills area after crossing Mackenzie Country farmland. The Tekapo–Pukaki Canal road crosses the lower reaches just above the Tekapo River confluence. There's a pleasant campsite under the willows and silver birches near this ford.

Season   First Saturday in November–30 April.

Mary Burn holds brown and rainbow trout in the 1.2–2 kg range with an occasional larger brown in the upper reaches above S.H.8. The first 500 m above the campsite are choked by willows; thereafter there is excellent water, with the river winding across exposed farmland. Fish can be stalked with a careful approach, and usually lie in the deeper corner pools. The stream is best fished either early or late in

The inaccessible Maitland River Gorge.

the season, the best water lying between the willows and the power pylons. It remains fishable when the Fork Stream is silt-laden. Both dry flies and sunk nymphs should be used; catch and release is recommended.

Fork Stream

Location and access   Flows parallel to, but east of, the Mary Burn and also joins the Tekapo River. Crossed by S.H.8 at the Tekapo Military Camp. Access to the lower reaches is from the Tekapo–Pukaki Canal road.

Season   First Saturday in November–30 April.

This stream holds browns and rainbows but is rather unstable and prone to flooding. It has tussock and matagouri banks and a shingle bed, and is best fished in December–January in the lower reaches.

Jollie River

Location and access   Follows a southerly course to join the Tasman River at the head of Lake Pukaki. Take the Braemar–Mt Cook Station road from Pukaki up the east side of the lake to Mt Cook Station where permission should be obtained.

The road crosses at a gorge above which there are a few pools and runs. Generally, however, the river is fast flowing and difficult to fish. There are willows in the lower reaches, but these do not greatly impede casting. Fish are hard to spot and the nor'wester often makes accurate casting difficult. A well-weighted nymph fished blind is the most effective method.

Lake Alexandrina

Location and access   Lies just west of the southern end of Lake Tekapo. Road access to the lake leaves S.H.8 3 km west of Tekapo on the Glenmore–Godley Peaks road. The turn-off to the lake is not signposted. Just before the turn-off to the Mt John Observatory there's a gate on the left and a rough track crosses farmland to the southern end of the lake and a fishing village.

Season   First Saturday in November–30 April.

Restrictions   No powerboats are permitted, nor is fishing from an unanchored boat within 200 m of the shore. The bag limit is 6 fish.

This is a very popular lake, especially with Timaru anglers, and there are fishing huts on the southern and eastern shore. Alexandrina, which lies in a tussock basin and has a willow-lined shore, holds browns and rainbow averaging 1–2 kg with an occasional fish up to 4 kg. Fish can be spotted only in clear, bright conditions, and blind lure fishing is generally the most popular method. Use Hamill's Killer, Mrs Simpson, Muddler Minnow, Yellow Dorothy, Parson's Glory, Kilwell or Rabbit lures on a medium-sinking line and fish over the lip or blue line round the lake edge. The area round the Island is a favourite location for boat fishing as there are some deep holes where rainbow trout tend to congregate. Use a deep-sinking line and lure.

Lake McGregor

Location   Lies between Lakes Alexandrina and Tekapo. The Glenmore–Godley Peaks road passes by the eastern shore.

Season   First Saturday in November–30 April.

Restrictions   Fly fishing only in this lake.

Lake Alexandrina drains into this lake, but fishing is prohibited in this creek. The lake is small and can be fished with a lure in similar fashion to Alexandrina. In the shallower water near the creek inlet and at the outlet, dry fly, lure and unweighted nymph fishing can bring results in favourable weather conditions.

Lake Tekapo

Location and access   This, the northernmost lake in the Upper Waitaki basin, has been harnessed for hydro-electric power. The Lilybank road follows up the eastern shore, S.H.8 passes the southern shore at Tekapo township, and the Glenmore–Godley Peaks road runs for some distance in close proximity to the western shore.

Season   Open all year.

Although in summer this lake is coloured by glacial flour brought down by the Godley River, trout can be caught. In winter when the glacial melt ceases, the lake is often much clearer. The eastern shore near the Lake McGregor outlet, the mouth of the Cass River and the Glenmore Station tarn outlet are well worth exploring either with a fly rod or spinning gear. In these areas the lake can clear sufficiently for spotting and stalking trout. The mouths of the Mistake and Macaulay rivers also yield fish.

Glenmore Station Tarn

Location   Take the farm track which leaves the Glenmore–Godley Peaks road opposite Lake Murray.

This tarn has been securely electrically fenced by the Department of Conservation to protect black stilt nests. Permission should be obtained from either the Department or Glenmore Station as there are times when fishing is permitted. The tarn holds good-sized rainbow and brown trout, which can be seen cruising the lake margins. Use a tiny, lightly weighted Hare and Copper nymph.

Fishing the Mary Burn in the Tekapo basin.

Cass River

Location   Drains the Hall and Gammack ranges, flows between these mountains in a southerly direction and enters Lake Tekapo just north of Lake Alexandrina.

Access   The Glenmore–Godley Peaks road crosses the lower reaches, but permission should be obtained from Glenmore or Godley Peaks Station to fish the middle reaches.

At the roadbridge the river is unstable, shingly and flood-prone — it can take a week to clear after heavy rain. Walk 2 km upstream to the gorge where there is good, stable water and some deep holes. This continues for 3 km upstream to the mouth of the Joseph Stream. The river again becomes unstable above this stream. It holds browns and rainbows which can be spotted in good conditions.

Boundary Stream

Location and access   Drains the Two Thumb Range and enters the eastern shore of Lake Tekapo. Access to the lower reaches from the Lilybank road.

This small, shingly stream is best fished early or late in the season. If one is prepared to tramp, then there are a few good resident browns in selected holes well upstream.

Macaulay River

Location and access   Joins the Godley River near Lilybank Station at the head of Lake Tekapo. Take the Lilybank road to the head of the lake.

Although the river floods easily there is a reasonable amount of holding water well upstream near the confluence with the North-east Gorge Stream. Access either by tramping or by jet boat providing there is sufficient water. The lower reaches above the mouth are worth exploring if the river is low and clear and the nor'wester kind. The Macaulay holds both brown and rainbow trout.

A few spring-fed side creeks further up the Godley River hold fish, but this is tramper's country and a visit for the fishing alone, despite the magnificent scenery, can hardly be recommended.

Coal River

Location   Drains the Two Thumb Range and the Round Hill Skifield and flows west into the head of Lake Tekapo.

Access   From Lake Tekapo take the Lilybank road following the eastern shore of Tekapo. The road to Lilybank Station crosses the river near the mouth just south of Mt Gerald Station, while the branch road to the Tekapo Skifield runs close to the river further upstream.

The middle and upper reaches are turbulent and difficult, but there are a few small unstable pools in the lower reaches worth fishing; the mouth is a favoured spot. A few large browns and smaller rainbows are present.

Otago District

Climatic conditions vary enormously within the Otago District. In West Otago the country is mountainous, remote and bush-clad with a rainfall in the region of 3 000 mm per year. In Central Otago, rainfall may be as little as 250 mm per year, and a number of rivers have been dammed to supply water for orchard irrigation. Coastal Otago's rainfall is greater at 600–1 200 mm per year. Hydro-electric generation schemes have modified a number of rivers, including the Clutha, Fraser, Teviot, Taieri and Waipori.

Brown trout were first introduced in 1869 and are now well established in most rivers. Sea-run browns provide sport at the mouths of the Shag, Waikouaiti, Taieri, Clutha and Catlins rivers. Rainbow trout were released about the turn of the century but have not thrived in Central and South Otago and are only present in Lake Mahinerangi and Manorburn Reservoir.

However, there are good stocks in the rivers and lakes of the Wanaka, Hawea and Wakatipu areas. Just as creeper fishing has played a significant and acceptable part in the trout fishing scene of Taranaki, so live-bait fishing is accepted in parts of Otago and Southland, and indeed is very popular in some of the lower reaches of rivers and their estuaries.

Unless otherwise specified, the season runs from 1 October to 30 April and the bag limit is 10 trout or salmon, but only 4 salmon may be taken, and only 4 trout from the Pomohaka River above Park Hill bridge. Minimum size is 25 cm.

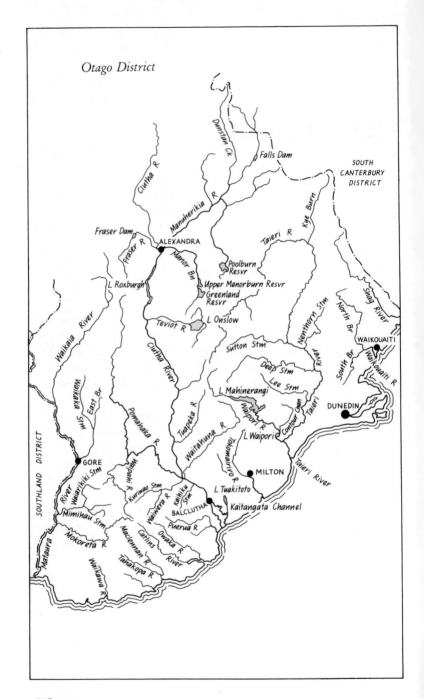

Otago District

Dunstan Ck

Falls Dam

SOUTH CANTERBURY DISTRICT

Clutha R

Manuherikia R

Kye Burn

Taieri R

Fraser Dam

Fraser R

ALEXANDRA

Manor Bn

Poolburn Resvr

Upper Manorburn Resvr

Greenland Resvr

L Roxburgh

L Onslow

Teviot R

Nenthorn Stm

Snag River

North Br

South Br

WAIKOUAITI

Waikouaiti R

Sutton Stm

Deep Stm

Lee Stm

Waikaia River

Clutha River

Tuapeka R

L Mahinerangi

Waipori R

Contour Chan

Taieri R

DUNEDIN

Pomahaka R

Waitahuna R

L Waipori

Waikaka Stm

East Br

Tokomairiro R

MILTON

SOUTHLAND DISTRICT

GORE

Waiparikiki Stm

Waipahi R

Kuriwao Stm

Waiwera R

Kaihiku Stm

L Tuakitoto

Taieri River

Mimihau Stm

Maclennan River

Puerua R

BALCLUTHA

Kaitangata Channel

Mataura

Mokoreta R

Catlins River

Owaka R

Tahakopa R

Waikawa R

North Otago
Shag River

> **Location and access**   This medium-sized river rises in the Kakanui
> Mountains, flows south-east and enters the Pacific Ocean at Shag
> Point just east of Palmerston. Access from S.H.1 for the lower reaches
> and estuary and from many side roads (Switchback, Munro, Jones,
> Craig, McLew and Limekiln) crossing the river that leave S.H.85
> from Palmerston to Dunback.
>
> **Season**   Open all year below S.H.1.

The upper reaches above Dunback flow through tussock and scrub
country, are not heavily fished and contain a few reasonable trout
only in selected holding pools. From Dunback to Palmerston the river
tends to be infested with willow and blackberry, but there are excellent
numbers of good fish up to 2.5 kg (44 takable fish/km found on drift
dives at Dunback) in the clear, slow-flowing water flowing over a
shingle, mud and weed bed. These can be spotted and stalked in summer
with small dry flies, nymphs, willow grub and midge pupa imitations.

Bank vegetation and clear, still water certainly make fly casting
testing, but there are selected spots where the river can be fished with
good results. Wading will disturb fish, but the river can be crossed
in selected places. In February, water flows decrease and weed growth
becomes a problem. The lower reaches and the estuary offer sea-run
fish early in the season when whitebait are running, and again late
in the season when fish run upstream to spawn. These can be taken
on silver and gold spinners and smelt flies.

Waikouaiti River

> **Location and access**   Rises in the steep, tussock-covered hills west
> of Waikouaiti. The north and south branches meet near Orbells
> Crossing, west of Cherry Farm Psychiatric Hospital, and enter the
> sea at Karitane. Access from S.H.1 on Ramrock Road just south
> of Waikouaiti, McGrath Road, Mill Road at Orbells Crossing and
> Kiatoa Road at Bucklands Crossing.
>
> **Season**   Open all year below S.H.1. Elsewhere, 1 October–30
> April.

This river has similar characteristics to the Shag. The lower reaches below the confluence of the two branches are sluggish, willow-lined, tidal and suitable for threadlining and bait fishing. Good sea-run fish can be caught late in the season on smelt flies. Above Orbells Crossing on the south branch and above Bucklands Crossing on the north branch there is reasonable fly fishing for the energetic angler provided you can avoid the willows. Fishing is best early in the season before low flows and weed growth make conditions difficult. There are some good picnic spots here.

South Otago

Taieri River

> **Location and access**   Rises in the high tussock country of the Lammerlaw Ranges of Central Otago, follows a northerly course to Waipiata, then bends south round the Rock and Pillar Range and enters the sea 30 km south of Dunedin.
>
> **Season**   Open all year downstream from the main roadbridge on S.H.1 at Allanton. Elsewhere, 1 October–30 April.

The river is more than 250 km in length and, for convenience, is here divided into three sections.

Upper reaches: From the headwaters to Waipiata

> **Access**   Many roads, including the Styx–Patearoa, Upper Taieri–Paerau, Puketoi–Patearoa, Patearoa–Maniototo and Patearoa–Ranfurly roads, give access to the river.

From well above Paerau to Waipiata, with the exception of a gorge at Hore's Bridge, the river follows a slow, convoluted course across the exposed, swampy Upper Taieri and Maniototo Plains. The river is slow-flowing, the water peat-stained, so fish are difficult to spot, yet they are reasonably plentiful. Access can be difficult in places because of swamp. In the gorge there are deep pools and fast runs which can be fished with a spinner. There are some good-sized browns in this section which respond to Coch-y-bondhu, Dark Red Spinner and Greenwell's Glory dry flies, Waterboatman (Corixa) imitations and unweighted nymphs. Live-bait and spinning methods also take fish. These upper reaches are not heavily fished.

Middle reaches: Waipiata to Outram

> **Access**   From S.H.87 and side roads off this highway.

Between Waipiata and Kokonga there is excellent accessible water for the fly angler. Between Kokonga and Hyde (Horseburn Road at Tiroiti) the river enters a rough gorge which can be negotiated in boots and shorts. From below Hyde to Sutton the river is willow-lined and flows over a shingle bed with pools and runs. There's reasonable fly fishing in this stretch. Fish can be taken by all legal angling methods. From Sutton to Outram the river again enters a deep gorge, which should only be tackled by fit anglers using spinning gear. The Mosgiel–Mt Allan road and the Outram–Hindon road give access to this gorge.

Lower reaches: Outram to Taieri Mouth

> **Access**   There are numerous roads in this area giving access to the river.

The river is tidal below Allanton and difficult to fish without a boat in the deep, gorgy, slow-flowing section below Henley Ferry. In summer the water can be disturbed by water-skiers. Between Outram and Allanton the river is willow-lined and has deep holes and a shingle bed. Trout can be taken in this section on lures, weighted nymphs and dry flies, but the river is somewhat polluted.

In the tidal section live bait accounts for most fish. Sea-run trout are caught at the mouth from September to November on smelt imitation flies fished across the current on a floating line and on spinners.

Taieri tributaries

There are a number of small tributaries, most of minor significance from an angling point of view. They include:

Kye Burn

This small tributary flows south from Kye Burn Diggings to join the Taieri near Kokonga. S.H.85 crosses at Kye Burn. As fish run up from the Taieri to spawn in this tributary, fishing is best either early or late in the season, mainly in a few deep holes in the lower reaches below S.H.85. In summer, water is removed for irrigation, the water warms up and it is not worth fishing.

Nenthorn Stream
This stream can be reached from the road running between Middlemarch and Macrae's Flat and various side roads off this route. The water is tea-coloured and most fish are taken on spinning gear.

Deep Stream
Access to this stream, which enters the Taieri above Hindon, is from the Outram–Middlemarch road (S.H.87) and then the road to Rocklands from Clarks Junction or Rocklands Road. This tea-coloured stream winds through tussock on a rock and stone bed and holds a few average-sized brown trout.

Lee Stream
S.H.87 crosses this stream at Traquair. There is reasonable 'blind' fly fishing upstream from S.H.87 in this tea-coloured stream. The heavily bushed gorge downstream from S.H.87 is rather inaccessible.

The gentle Pomahaka River near Conical Hill.

146

Lower Waipori River
(See Central Otago section for Lake Mahinerangi.)
Access is from S.H.1 on the Henley–Berwick–Waipori Falls road. This river has been severely modified for power generation. However, the section of river in the Waipori Gorge, although subject to fluctuating flows, holds good brown trout in attractive bush surroundings. Fly fishing, threadlining and bait fishing can all be effective, but fish this section in boots and shorts.

Below the gorge the river is tidal and rather uninteresting although it does hold trout and is open for fishing all year. The Lower Waipori eventually joins the Taieri at Henley Ferry bridge.

Lakes Waihola and Waipori also hold fish but are not highly regarded, fished mainly by local residents with live bait.

Tokomairiro River

Location and access   The east and west branches of this small stream flow south-east through the township of Milton and join just south of this town. S.H.1 crosses both branches just south of Milton. Access to the west branch is from S.H.8 at Glenore and Mt Stuart; the east branch is reached from the Milton–Tablehill road and north branch road off S.H.1.

Season   Open all year only below Coal Gully roadbridge. Elsewhere, 1 October–30 April.

This small stream flowing across farmland becomes sluggish and weedy downstream from Milton. It used to be heavily polluted by woolscouring run-off, but this ceased some years ago and the river has now recovered to some extent. It holds small brown trout and most are taken on spinners and live bait in the lower reaches. The branches offer limited small-stream fly fishing early in the season.

Lower Clutha and tributaries

Lower Clutha River
The Upper Clutha is described in this chapter under 'Lakes Wanaka, Hawea and surrounding district'. The river below the Kawarau River confluence is usually silt-laden from the Shotover and Arrow rivers and has been extensively modified for hydro-electric power generation.

This section refers to that stretch of water from below the Roxburgh Dam to the mouth.

> **Access**   The river divides below Balclutha into the Matau and Koau branches. There is good access from roads in the region of Inch Clutha.
>
> **Season**   Open all year below S.H.1 at Balclutha.

Both branches flow in a deep channel between stopbanks. This very large, high-volume river is heavily fished, mainly by live-bait and threadline anglers, and the catch rate is surprisingly high all year round despite fluctuating flows due to hydro control. During the summer the tidal reaches yield large, sea-run trout to imitation smelt lures and silver and gold spinners. There's a small run of quinnat salmon in February–March. The river upstream from Balclutha is willow-infested and a boat is required. Water-skiers can be disturbing.

Waiwera River

> **Location and access**   Drains the Kaihiku Range and flows north to enter the Clutha on its true right bank downstream from Clydevale. S.H.1 crosses the river 15 km west of Balclutha and east of Clinton. Kuriwao Siding Road, Hillfoot Road and Waiwera Gorge Road offer access to the river although a walk across farmland is usually required.

Below S.H.1 the river is overgrown with willows. At S.H.1, the river appears sluggish and uninviting. Upstream, however, there's good water, especially in the gorge, holding browns averaging 1 kg that respond to small weighted upstream nymphs or dry flies. It is best fished early in the season before weed growth becomes a problem.

Pomahaka River

> **Location and access**   Rises in the Umbrella Mountains south of Roxburgh and winds for 125 km through West Otago to enter the Clutha below Clydevale not far from the mouth of the Waiwera River. There's good road access to most of the river.

For convenience, the river is divided into two sections.

Upper Pomahaka (above Switzers or Park Hill bridge)

Access   From roads north-east of Kelso, Tapanui and Heriot. Take Old Switzers Road to Park Hill Domain, Hukarere Station Road, Spylaw Burn Road or Aitcheson's Runs Road to Hamiltons Flat.

Restrictions   The bag limit is 4 trout above Park Hill bridge.

The river meanders across attractive but exposed barren tussock country. There are some deep pools, but the water is clear flowing over a rock and stone bed and fish can be spotted. In February–March, large browns up to 4.5 kg arrive in this area to spawn. They respond to sunk nymphs, dry flies and black lures fished deep through the holes after dark.

On one of my visits to this area I tried to get downstream of a large brown hanging in the current behind a rock, but made the mistake of climbing too high up the bank. There was no cover in the tussock and when I had achieved my objective the fish had gone. It was the only fish I saw on that occasion.

Middle and lower reaches

Access
Middle reaches   From the Waipahi-Conical Hill road which parallels the river near the Conical Hill sawmill. The Waikoikoi road crosses between Tapanui and Conical Hill.
Lower reaches   From Burkes Ford Road, Ross Road, Taumata Road, the Clinton–Clydevale road and the Waiwera–Clydevale road at Black's bridge.

There is a wide variety of water in these sections. Dusky Forest offers rough boots-and-shorts fishing. Between Kelso and Tapanui the river enters a fishable gorge; from Tapanui to Conical Hill, it winds across farmland and becomes willow-lined, weedy and slower-flowing, holding fish averaging 1.2 kg. Downstream from Conical Hill, the river soon becomes swift and the banks choked with willows, and fish cannot be spotted in the tea-coloured water. There are stretches of water that can be fished, however, the middle reaches being the most heavily fished, with many anglers preferring to spin. The lower reaches are slow-flowing and deep and although fly anglers catch fish, many use live bait and spinners.

Waipahi River

Location and access   Rises from swampy tussock country west of Clinton and winds its way across open swampy farmland generally in a northerly direction to join the Pomahaka River south of Conical Hill. S.H.1 crosses the river at Arthurton and Webb Road off S.H.1 leads to the lower reaches. The Clinton–Gore back road crosses higher up while the road to Wyndham leaves from this crossing and generally follows the river upstream.

As a novice teenage fly fisherman, I remember being puzzled by two flies in a Christchurch sports shop, the Waipahi Red and Black. These flies had their origins on this river. The Waipahi is highly regarded as a fly stream holding browns averaging around 1 kg, and fishes best early and late in the season as weed growth from eutrophication causes problems in high summer.

Fish are not easy to spot in the slightly tea-coloured water, so blind fishing the runs or fishing to rising fish is advised. There's a local annual fishing competition on this river at the end of October called the Gold Medal Event. Try Hare and Copper and Pheasant Tail nymphs, Midge Pupa imitation or Dad's Favourite, Kakahi Queen and Greenwell's Dark dry flies in sizes 16–18. Waipahi Red and Black dry and wet flies might prove useful though I've never used them.

Owaka River

Location and access   Small river rising from the Wisp Range which flows south-east across farmland and empties into the lower end of the Catlins River at Pounawea just above Catlins Lake. S.H.92 crosses east of Owaka while the Owaka–Clinton road follows up the river.

Season   Open all year only below the Pounawea Rd–Newhaven roadbridge.

The Owaka, a small stream that discolours easily after rain, holds a few brown trout in the 0.75–1.3 kg range. Trout respond to all legal methods but are difficult to spot. Spinners and live bait take most fish. The stream is rather polluted by farming operations and should be fished early in the season.

Catlins River

Location and access   Drains the Beresford and Wisp ranges and swampland in the Wisp area, flows south-east through the Catlins State Forest Park to empty into the tidal Catlins Lake south of Owaka. S.H.92 crosses the river just above Catlins Lake, but the river is slow-flowing and tidal. Take the Owaka–Clinton road and turn off onto Morris Saddle Road. This leads to an excellent camping area at the Tawanui Recreation Reserve. The Chloris Pass road, off the Clinton–Owaka road, leads to the upper reaches. There are also forestry tracks through the Catlins Forest Park that lead to good stretches of water.

Season   Open all year below the S.H.92 roadbridge. Elsewhere, 1 October–30 April.

The Catlins is a very scenic river holding brown trout averaging 1–2 kg, but it's rather difficult to fish. The upper reaches flow across open country above Wisp Station and offer testing dry fly and nymph fishing, especially early and late in the season. There are some good deep holes, though fish are difficult to spot in the tea-coloured water. In the Catlins State Forest Park the water is deep in the pools, dark and slow-flowing but holds a reasonable stock of fish. Again, fish cannot be spotted.

Upstream from Tawanui in the region of Franks Creek there is excellent fly water, though most fish are taken on spinners. Try mayfly imitations such as Dad's Favourite, Kakahi Queen and Twilight Beauty or well-weighted nymphs such as Hare and Copper in sizes 10–14. Below Tawanui the river is sluggish and best suited to spinning or live-bait fishing. The tidal Catlins Lake holds sea-run trout that can be taken on spinners, smelt flies and live bait, but a boat is necessary. Some good fish are taken at night in high summer.

Tahakopa River

Location and access   Rises from Table Ridge in the Catlins State Forest Park, flows south-east and empties into Tahakopa Bay. Access from the Tahakopa Valley road.

Season   Open all year below the Maclennan confluence.

This is another scenic, tea-stained river, similar to the Catlins but smaller and more remote. Fish respond to nymphs, dry flies and spinners.

The Maclennan tributary also holds fish but, as with the Tahakopa, fish are not easy to spot.

Central Otago

Lake Mahinerangi

> **Location and access**   Formed by damming the Waipori River for hydro-electric power generation. Access from S.H.87 on Mahinerangi Road, the Waipori Falls road and from S.H.8 at Lawrence on the Lawrence–Waipori road.

Mahinerangi is a large, exposed lake, subject to fluctuating water levels, holding brown and rainbow trout and perch. It has a clear, grassy shoreline except where forestry clothes the western shore. Fish cannot be spotted but rise to dry flies and accept sunk lures, spinners and live bait. I recently took a good-condition brown weighing 1.3 kg on a Coch-y-bondhu dry fly. At times, a cicada imitation can be deadly.

Manuherikia River

> **Location and access**   Rises in the dry tussock-covered St Bathans Range close to Lindis Pass and flows down the Manuherikia Valley south to join the Clutha River at Alexandra. The lower, willow-choked reaches lie some distance east of S.H.85 between Alexandra and Ophir and a long walk across farmland is necessary to reach the river. S.H.85, Loop Road and Fiddlers Flat Road closely follow the river from Becks to Falls Dam.

The middle and lower reaches can be low, warm and clear in the hot Central Otago summers as water is drawn off for irrigation. The river is willow-lined and braided and flows over a shingle bed. Despite the low catch rate and the river's not being highly rated in this area, reasonable numbers of medium-sized brown trout have been seen near Ophir on drift dives (75 fish/km). However, the best water lies east of St Bathans, both below and in the gorge below Falls Dam, where there is the chance of a good fish for the energetic boots-and-shorts angler.

Falls Dam

Location and access   Lying east of St Bathans, it was formed by damming the Manuherikia River for irrigation. Reached by Fiddlers Flat Road to the lower end and Home Hills Runs Road to the top end.

Falls Dam holds browns in the 0.75–1.5 kg range that cannot be spotted but can be taken on fliers, spinners and live bait. The top end of the dam has become rather silted up, but these shallows provide good fishing near the mouth of the Upper Manuherikia River, especially at night with a black sunk lure of the Mrs Simpson type.

Butchers Dam

Location and access   S.H.8 6 km south of Alexandra skirts the western shore.

Season   Open all year.

This shallow lake holds browns in the 0.75–1.2 kg range. Fish can be spotted cruising in the shallow inlets and will accept dry flies and unweighted nymphs in sizes 14–16. A low, careful approach is required.

Conroys Dam

Location and access   Lies almost on the opposite side of S.H.8 from Butchers Dam and, like Butchers, is used for irrigation. Take Conroys Road off Earnscleugh Road, then a Ministry of Works road to the dam.

Season   Open all year.

This is another shallow lake, similar to Butchers Dam, holding small brown trout. Try Coch-y-bondhu or a cicada imitation.

Frasers Dam

Location and access   Cross the Clutha at Alexandra and turn right onto Earnscleugh Road, then to the end of Blackman Road.

Similar to Butchers and Conroys dams.

The upper Fraser River, flowing into the top end of the dam, is worth exploring with a weighted nymph by the energetic angler in boots and shorts.

Upper Manorburn Reservoir

Location and access   From Galloway north-east of Alexandra take the Crawford Hills road and turn right onto the Ministry of Works road to the fishermen's huts at the dam, about 40 km from Alexandra. Boat-launching facilities are available.

Season   1 November–30 April.

This large, deep dam contains only rainbows in the 1–1.5 kg range. Fish cannot be spotted but will accept flies, spinners and live bait.

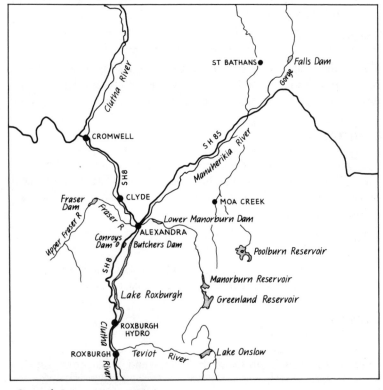

Central Otago rivers and dams

Poolburn Reservoir

> **Location and access**   Turn off at Galloway north-east of Alexandra and take the road to Moa Creek. From Moa Creek take the signposted Old Dunstan Road to the reservoir.
>
> **Season**   Open all year.

Poolburn holds browns that can be caught on live bait, spinners, wet and dry flies and lures. It tends to become shallow and weedy in summer and fish are difficult to spot.

Lake Onslow

> **Location and access**   Lies east of Roxburgh and south of the Manorburn Reservoir. Take Wright, Sanders and Lake Onslow roads from Roxburgh East to the lake. There's a boat ramp at the outlet.
>
> **Season**   Open all year.

Formed by the damming of the Teviot River, this hydro lake, covering over 800 ha, lies in barren tussock country so typical of Central Otago and holds brown trout which cannot be spotted round the lake edge. All fishing methods can be successful and an occasional fish up to 3.5 kg can be anticipated. It's best fished from a boat by trolling with a spinner.

The Teviot River contains small brown trout but has been severely modified for hydro generation.

Lakes Wanaka and Hawea and surrounding district

> **Season**   For all rivers and their tributaries flowing into Lakes Wanaka and Hawea, 1 November–31 May. This includes the Makarora, Young, Wilkin, Albert Burn, Matukituki, Hunter, Dingle and Timaru rivers. For Lakes Wanaka and Hawea, 1 October–30 September.
>
> **Restrictions**   The bag limit for these lakes is 6 fish; for the rivers flowing into Wanaka and Hawea, 3 fish.

Makarora River

Location and access   Rises near the Haast Pass, drains the Young Range and flows down a wide tussock valley to enter Lake Wanaka south of Makarora. S.H.6 follows the river from where it emerges from a gorge above Davis Flat to Lake Wanaka.

Although this river holds browns and rainbows throughout its length only the upper reaches above the confluence with the Young River can be recommended to the fly angler. Below this point, even though fish can be caught, the river is unstable, braided, shingly and prone to changing course in a flood. It is suitable for spinning. However, the most interesting water for the fly angler lies at Cameron, Kiwi and Davis flats, where fish can be seen in stable, clear water conditions. Stocks are not great as the river offers easy access from the main road and is heavily fished. Landlocked quinnat salmon from Lake Wanaka spawn in this river in winter.

The lower reaches of Camerons Creek hold a few fish, and if you are keen on rock climbing the Fish River is worth exploring.

The Blue River has an impassable gorge near the Makarora confluence which prevents trout from ascending this beautiful valley.

Young River

Location and access   Joins the Makarora 4 km downstream from the Blue River. The access track leaves S.H.6 at Brady's Creek and crosses farmland to the Makarora–Young confluence. Beware of the Makarora crossing! One can usually find a suitable ford at the tail of a pool in low-water conditions either above or below the confluence of the two rivers. The track follows the river upstream on the true left bank.

The Young holds mainly rainbow. The lower 1.5 km holds the odd fish, but in the gorge fish can clearly be seen from the track high up on the true left bank, in short deep pools protected by large boulders. They present a real challenge to 'rock climbing' anglers, but I have never been able to walk past these trout without casting a fly. Landing one of these fish is another story! The best fishing is around the junction of the north and south branches; anglers intending to tramp this far may need to camp. It's a 2- to 3-hour tramp to the forks.

There's also excellent fishing for 1 km up the north branch before a formidable gorge blocks progress; there are no fish in the south branch. The fish are not large but present a challenge in very clear mountain water. Catch and release strongly recommended in this highly regarded river as stocks are not high. It is best fished in February and March. Try Coch-y-bondhu, Greenwell's Glory, Mole Fly and Twilight Beauty dry flies or weighted Hare and Copper, Red Tipped Governor, Pheasant Tail and Half Back nymphs in sizes 12–16. If the westerly makes casting upstream difficult, try fishing the pools with Yellow Rabbit or Red Setter lures on a medium-sinking line in sizes 6–8.

Wilkin River

Location and access   This is the largest of the three tributaries, all of which flow on a parallel course and enter the true right bank of the Makarora River. The Wilkin enters about 9 km above Lake Wanaka. Both the Makarora and the Wilkin rivers need to be forded and this can indeed be hazardous in anything but low-water summer conditions. However, the shingly riverbed is not slippery. The Makarora crossing is best above the confluence with the Wilkin and this river should then be followed up the true left bank.

Anglers are strongly advised to seek information on the state of the rivers from the ranger station or the store at Haast Pass Tourist Service. A jet boat service operates on the Wilkin and bookings can be made at the store. If anglers intend to ford the rivers and tramp, information can be obtained from *Moir's Guidebook* or *A Tramper's Guide to New Zealand's National Parks*.

February and March are the best fishing months in this area, when rivers are most likely to be low and clear. The lower reaches are unstable with shifting silt, but at Kerin Forks there's excellent water of the rock and stone type containing pools and runs overhung by beech trees. Fly anglers should travel at least 12 km upstream before fishing. It's 16 km to the Parks Board hut at Kerin Forks.

Fish are not easy to spot in the turbulent water and deep blue pools, but blind fishing with a weighted nymph or downstream lure methods can provide exciting sport for both browns and rainbows. This beautiful valley, with tussock flats, beech bush and towering snow-capped mountains, is very popular with trampers.

I first fished the Wilkin many years ago and swapped trout for venison and camp-oven bread with two deer cullers. My fishing companion spent five days fishing a single pool and landed 6 fish, including a 4 kg brown.

The Siberia Stream, which joins the Wilkin at Kerin Forks, also offers excellent fly water, but catch and release methods are strongly recommended as this water can easily be cleaned out. The Siberia cattle track follows up the true left bank from Kerin Forks and climbs steeply up into the bush for 400 m before descending to the Siberia Flats. There's a fixed-wing airstrip on the Siberia Flats.

Albert Burn

Location and access   Flows into Lake Wanaka on the western shore 8 km from the head of the lake. Access is usually by boat, though energetic tramper/anglers can cross the Makarora River in low-water summer conditions and tramp along the lake shore to the mouth.

Fishing water is limited, with only the lower 2 km of river below the gorge holding fish, but here it is a good, clear, rock- and stone-type mountain stream offering excellent fly water where fish can be stalked. As with the Wilkin, the best fishing is in February–March.

Matukituki River

Location and access   Drains Mt Aspiring and surrounding mountains. From the confluence of the east and west branches the river follows a south-easterly course and enters Lake Wanaka at West Wanaka. Take the road from Wanaka to Glendhu Bay and on through Hell's Gate. The West Wanaka road branches off to the right and leads to a swingbridge across the lower reaches and an angler's access, while the Mt Aspiring road leads upstream through Cattle Flat Station to the junction of the west and east branches. There's an emergency four-wheel-drive track to the Aspiring Hut.

I have a soft spot for this river, having caught my first fish on a fly in the west branch at the age of 14. I cast a Taupo Tiger lure upstream which failed to sink and a rainbow rose and took it for a dry fly! Although there are both browns and rainbows in the main river, it is large, shingly, unstable and best suited to spinning. Fly anglers should tramp up either branch as both hold fish in reasonably stable water. Though the east branch can be discoloured by glacial flour it is usually clear and fish can be spotted and stalked up as far as Junction Flat. The west branch holds fish almost up to Aspiring Hut. Stocks are not high, but the scenery compensates for this. At the end of the season, trout entering the mouth and lower reaches to spawn will accept a sunk lure fished across and down with the current.

The Motutapu River, which enters the Matukituki at Cattle Flat, holds a few rainbow. The Motutapu road behind Glendhu Bay camp follows Jack Halls Creek through private land to the middle reaches and a gorge where there are always a few fish.

Lake Wanaka

Access   Road access to many areas of this large lake is somewhat limited and some of the best fishing spots can only be reached by boat. The road to Glendhu Bay and West Wanaka generally runs within walking distance of the shore. S.H.6 follows the eastern shore from the head of the lake to The Neck. Aubrey, Beacon Point, Maungawera and Dublin Bay roads give limited access in the vicinity of Wanaka township. There are boat-launching facilities at Wanaka and Glendhu Bay, and Camp and Wharf streams up the eastern side of the lake.

Wanaka holds brown and rainbow trout and landlocked quinnat salmon. Most fish are taken by trolling or spinning from the shore. Stevensons Arm, the Makarora and Matukituki deltas and Glendhu Bay are good trolling areas. Varieties of Cobra and Toby, Tasmanian Devil, Flatfish and Zed spinners will all take fish. During the winter months use lead line as fish will be feeding on the bottom. Cruising trout can also be stalked along the shoreline.
   Paddock Bay, reached from the West Wanaka road via an angler's access, is a favoured fly fishing area. The bay is shallow and weedy with sandy patches, and fish cruise in close to the shore. During the day, try a small wet fly or lure such as a Muddler Minnow on a floating line or an unweighted nymph such as Hare's Ear or Pheasant Tail. Cast well ahead of cruising fish or even let your fly sink onto a sandy patch and activate it when a trout cruises within range. At dusk, Dad's Favourite, Kakahi Queen and Twilight Beauty dry flies will all take fish.
   If the lake is high, try the shallow inlets near the willows towards

the southern end of the bay. Fish cruise close to shore beneath the willows, especially towards dusk. Large cruising fish can usually be seen from the top of Glendhu Bluff on the roadside near Hell's Gate, but there's no access to the water here.

Lake Hawea

Access S.H.6 follows the western shore from The Neck to the outlet at Hawea. The steep and narrow road to Dingle Burn Station follows the eastern shore but generally runs high above the lake. Boat-launching facilities are available at the Hawea motor camp.

This lake was raised for power generation, but fishing is still good, especially from a boat or by spinning from the shore for browns, rainbows and landlocked quinnat salmon. Hot spots are The Neck, the mouth of Timaru Creek, the Hunter River delta and Silver Island. Cruising trout in the shallower bays can be enticed with flies in similar fashion to those in Lake Wanaka.

Hunter River

Location and access Rises from the Bealey Range of the Main Divide near the source of the Wills River. From The Forks in the headwaters, the valley follows a southerly direction for 30 km before entering Lake Hawea. Access is usually by jet boat. There's a four-wheel-drive track through Hunter Valley Station to Long Flat Creek, but the owners don't encourage its use as it is risky in all but good weather conditions. There are two fixed-wing airstrips in the valley, one at Forbes Hut, but their state of repair will vary. It is a 16-hour tramp from Hunter Valley Station to Forbes Hut.

This large river flows down a very long valley. In the lower reaches fishing is best by spinning or using a downstream lure. From Long Flat Creek (Ferguson Hut) to The Forks (Forbes Hut) the river is more confined and stable and there is excellent fly water. Both rainbows and browns up to 4 kg can be caught on dry fly, nymph and lure. The valley is exposed to the nor'westers which sweep down with great frequency, frustrating upstream fly anglers. In these conditions it is best to fish downstream with a sunk lure such as Parson's Glory, Yellow Rabbit, Muddler Minnow or Hamill's Killer. At night, try a Hairy

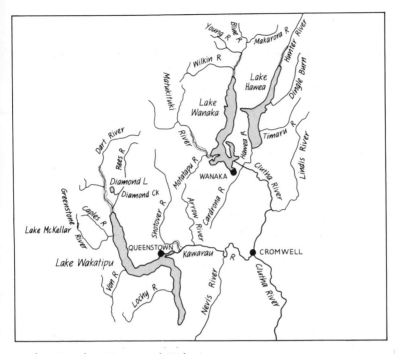

Lakes Wanaka, Hawea and Wakatipu

Dog or Mrs Simpson in some of the larger holes using a slow retrieve. This river deserves its high reputation despite being inaccessible.

Dingle Burn

Location and access Drains the mountains to the east of Lake Hawea, flows in a south-westerly direction and enters the lake north of Silver Island. Access to the mouth is by boat or on the Timaru River road to Dingle Burn Station. Permission should be obtained from the station when approaching the river from the lower reaches. Tramper/anglers can cross into the upper reaches from the Ahuriri River Valley above Birchwood Station. There's a marked horse-track winding up the hill on the south side of the upper Ahuriri River near the start of the bush. It's a three-hour tramp to the Dingle over a high saddle, but the views are magnificent. Many visiting anglers fly in by fixed-wing aircraft or helicopter.

This excellent remote nymphing stream flowing between high, bush-clad mountains is very popular with guides and their clients. It tends to be overfished, however, and catch and release is strongly advocated. Most fish now seem to have been caught more than once! The most accessible water lies between Cotters and the Upper Dingle huts. Here the valley opens out into tussock flats lined by beech forest.

This small river holds mainly rainbow averaging 1–2 kg in fast-flowing rocky pools and runs. Fish can usually be spotted, but the fast pocket water should not be ignored, especially in warm summer weather. The gorge in the lower reaches is formidable in anything but low-water summer conditions. However, there are some big fish in deep blue pools under the beech bush. Any small weighted nymph or buoyant dry fly should take fish, though some fish have become cunning after having been caught before.

The Dingle Lagoon near the mouth of the Dingle Burn on Dingle Burn Station holds brook char (fontinalis), some apparently of trophy size.

Timaru River

> **Location and access**   Flows on a course roughly parallel to the Dingle Burn but south of that river. The mouth is 20 km from Hawea on the Timaru River road which crosses the river at the Peter Muir bridge. Camping is permitted in this area.

The lower reaches are gorgy and generally contain small fish. About 3 km upstream from the mouth, the valley widens and becomes most attractive with tussock flats and patches of beech bush. The stream is clear, fish can be spotted with the aid of polaroids, and providing the weather is hot and still, the river is a delight for the dry fly and nymph angler. It holds browns and rainbows, the latter more prolific in November and December when there is a late spawning run.

Hawea River

> **Location and access**   Drains Lake Hawea and flows on a tortuous south-westerly course for 16 km before joining the Clutha River below Albert Town. There is good access below the Albert Town bridge on S.H.6 and from the Hawea Flat, Newcastle and Camp

Hill roads. The river flows beneath high river terraces, but access is available to both banks. Beware the briar roses!

Season 1 October–30 September.

Restrictions The bag limit is 6 fish.

The Hawea has been modified for hydro-electric generation, a weir having been built at the outlet, so watch for fluctuating flows. It generally remains constant during summer, however, and holds brown and rainbow trout up to 3.5 kg that can be taken on dry flies, nymphs and sunk dark lures fished at night. This river offers good fishing close to the townships of Wanaka and Hawea.

Clutha River (upper reaches)

Location and access Drains Lake Wanaka and flows south to Cromwell. There are many access points from Beacon Point Road, off the Dublin Bay road, and from Albert Town and Luggate, off S.H.6, S.H.8A and S.H.8. A favourite stretch at Deans Bank can be reached from the end of Alison Avenue at Albert Town. In places private farmland needs to be crossed to some of the best water, so please obtain permission.

Season 1 October–31 May. Below the Luggate bridge there's an open season from 1 October–30 September.

Restrictions The bag limit is 6 fish. Fly fishing only from the outlet to 600 m above the Albert Town bridge.

This very large river has the highest flow rate of any New Zealand river, and is not easy to fish. Draining a lake, the upper reaches are stable and remain clear even after heavy rain. There's a very high population of browns and rainbows, especially between the outlet and Albert Town. Drift dives have established that this river near the outlet holds the highest biomass (kg/km) of fish of any New Zealand river, at 275 fish/km.

Fish respond to spinning methods and fly fishing of all varieties, including downstream lures on a high-density line. As the water is heavy and the fish often lie deep during the day, try a well-weighted nymph on a sink-tipped line. Trout are not easy to spot but will rise freely late in the evenings during favourable conditions.

Sedge fishing on warm summer nights can be most exciting as fish will move into the shallows where they are more accessible. Fish across and down using a floating line with either a sparsely dressed wet fly such as March Brown, Purple Grouse, Red Tipped Governor or Twilight Beauty or an imitation sedge such as deer-hair patterns, Thompson's Moth, Turkey Sedge or Cinnamon Sedge. Sensitivity is required when using this method so tighten as soon as you feel a strike. If you are late, the deception is rapidly rejected. A large night lure such as Hairy Dog, Fuzzy Wuzzy, Green Maribou or Mrs Simpson can also bring results.

Lindis River

Location and access   Drains the Lindis Pass and runs parallel to S.H.8 to enter the Clutha below Tarras.

Season   1 October–31 May.

This very attractive willow-lined stream unfortunately holds very few fish. There are a few browns in the lower reaches near Tarras, with access across private farmland. The river dries in summer when water is taken for irrigation. It's the spawning stream for the Clutha.

Lake Wakatipu and surrounding district

Season   1 October–31 July for Lakes Hayes, Johnson, Kilpatrick, Moke, Dispute, Luna and Reid. All streams and rivers flowing into Lake Wakatipu, 1 November–31 May. For Lake Wakatipu the season is open all year.

Restrictions   The bag limit in Lake Wakatipu is 6 fish but only 3 fish in all rivers flowing into the lake.

Lake Wakatipu

Location and access   From Queenstown and Frankton, by boat and from S.H.6 to Kingston and the Glenorchy road.

Season   Open all year.

Fast-flowing Dingle Burn can offer exciting angling.

A very large, deep, scenic lake surrounded by high mountains, Wakatipu holds browns, rainbows and landlocked quinnat salmon. I have never enjoyed fishing this lake as there are few shallow inlets, but trollers and spin anglers take their share of fish. In selected places, especially off the Glenorchy road, fish can be spotted cruising, and stream mouths are worth trying at night with a slowly retrieved sunk night lure such as Fuzzy Wuzzy, Hairy Dog and Mrs Simpson.

Lake Hayes

Location and access   From the Queenstown–Arrowtown road.

Season   Open all year.

Lake Hayes holds good stocks of browns averaging 1–2 kg and perch. Shoreline fishing is limited because of willow infestation, and powerboats are prohibited. A rowing boat or float tube improves access. Try harling a bully-type lure such as Muddler Minnow, Mrs Simpson or Hamill's Killer on a high-density fly line. Be prepared for swimmers and yachts in summer.

Close by Lake Johnson holds rainbow and perch. Take Hansen Road opposite the Frankton golf course to this lake.

Lakes Kilpatrick and Moke

> **Location and access**   The road to these small lakes branches off the Glenorchy road some 7 km from Queenstown.

Kilpatrick, small and shallow and lying in a tussock basin, holds a good stock of cunning browns that can be seen and stalked with a dry fly or lightly weighted nymph. The most favoured shore lies away from the road.

Moke is deeper and larger and perhaps more difficult as fish are not easy to spot along the narrow shoreline. There's an attractive bush-covered peninsula where a green beetle imitation dry fly is worth trying. Elsewhere the shore comprises tussock, matagouri, briar rose and even a few red currants. Fish will rise to a Coch-y-bondhu, Dad's Favourite or Twilight Beauty or even accept a bully-type lure fished deep if the lake is rough.

Lake Dispute

> **Location and access**   A 25-minute walking track to this lake is marked on the Glenorchy road 3 km up the lake from the Moke Lake road.

This swampy, reedy lake lying in a tussock and matagouri basin holds brown trout and fontinalis which fight vigorously when hooked.

Lake Luna

> **Location and access**   The walking track to this lake starts near Mt Creighton Station. It's a two- to three-hour walk to the lake.

Luna holds browns which will surface in fascinating style from deep water to take dry flies.

Diamond Lake

> **Location and access**   Lies 15 km north of Glenorchy at the head of Lake Wakatipu near Paradise. The road reaches the eastern shore.
>
> **Season**   1 October–30 September.
>
> **Restrictions**   The bag limit is 6 fish.

This very scenic lake holds mainly browns, but there are a few rainbow and landlocked quinnat. Fish cruise the shallow, weedy bays and can be stalked with a dry fly or unweighted nymph provided the prevailing nor'wester does not blow you away.

Diamond Creek

Access   There's signposted angler's access over a stile soon after crossing the Rees River on the Glenorchy–Paradise road. Use the stile or run the risk of being zapped by the electric fence.

Season   1 November–31 March because landlocked quinnat salmon spawn in this stream.

Restrictions   The bag limit is 3 fish.

This creek drains Diamond and Reid lakes, flows against the base of a bush-clad hill and enters the Rees River. It's only 5 km long but offers clear water and one tussock bank where fish can easily be seen and will just as easily see you! It's a beautiful stream to fish in ideal conditions, having a weed and stone bed. Upstream fishing becomes impossible in a nor'wester, which also roughens the lake and discolours the stream.

Reid Lake, just south of Diamond Lake, also holds browns. The Rees and Routeburn rivers in this area hold fish but are not highly recommended as they are flood-prone and unstable.

Greenstone and Caples Rivers

Location and access   Drain the Livingstone, Ailsa and Humboldt mountains and Lake McKellar. Join 6 km from their mouth and enter the western side of Lake Wakatipu north of Elfin Bay. Access is by boat or south from Kinloch on the rough-metalled Greenstone Station road. There's a parking area at the start of the Greenstone–Caples Track at the road end.

Season   1 November–31 May.

Restrictions   The bag limit is 3 fish. Fly fishing only.

These are highly regarded mountain rivers holding browns and rainbows up to 4 kg in clear pools and runs. Fishing pressure has increased following road access so be prepared to tramp upstream to the best water in the middle reaches. There's plenty of it as the Greenstone alone offers 30 km of fishable water. Catch and release is recommended. The Caples Valley is worth visiting for the scenery alone, but the fishing can also be superb, especially early in the season. You will meet plenty of trampers.

Lake Rere to the south holds browns but because of overhanging bush is difficult to fish from the shore except with a spinner.

Von River

Location and access   Drains the Thomson Mountains and flows on a northerly course from the branch confluence to enter the western shore of Wakatipu just north of Whites Bay near Mt Nicholas Station. Access is by boat or by road on the Mavora Lakes and Mt Nicholas roads beyond the Mavora Lakes.

Season   1 November–31 May.

Restrictions   The bag limit is 3 fish. Fly fishing only.

A typical West Otago high-country stream flowing down a tussock valley, the Von holds browns and rainbows averaging 1.5 kg in clear pools and runs. It is best fished early in the season. Fish respond to all methods of fly fishing, but fishing has fallen off since road access has become available.

Lochy River

Location and access   Rises in the Eyre Mountains and follows a north-easterly course to enter Lake Wakatipu at Halfway Bay. Access is by boat or by tramping across mountainous tussock country from the Mt Nicholas road.

Season   1 November–31 May.

Restrictions   Fly fishing only. The bag limit is 3 fish.

The Lochy is another excellent high-country river holding mainly rainbows up to 2 kg. There's at least 20 km of fishable water upstream from the mouth, but the best water lies above where the Cecil Peak road meets the river and fishing continues upstream as far as

Killiecrankie Creek. There's a horse track up the true left bank. Fish will accept dry flies, nymphs or sunk lures. Try Coch-y-bondhu, Royal Wulff, Black Gnat and Palmer varieties, including Mole Fly dry flies, Pheasant Tail, Hare and Copper and Stonefly nymphs and Rabbit patterns, and Taupo Tiger or Yellow Dorothy lures. This highly recommended but inaccessible river is best fished in boots and shorts. Catch and release is recommended though you would be doing well to catch 2 or 3 fish a day.

Kawarau River
Reached on the road from Frankton to the Lake Wakatipu outlet, this large, clear, deep river doesn't hold many fish and is suitable for threadlining. It becomes discoloured only below the Shotover confluence, but the water is constantly disturbed by jet boats, so it is not highly recommended.

There are small trout in the Arrow River near Arrowtown, but the river is unstable and not highly regarded.

Roaring Meg dams
The rough Roaring Meg Stream enters the Kawarau River 10 km up the Kawarau Gorge from Cromwell. The river has two hydro dams

Diamond Creek at the head of Lake Wakatipu.

which can be reached on a shingle road. Both hold brown and rainbow trout but are difficult to fish because of steep shorelines. The water is therefore best suited to spinning methods.

Nevis River

Location and access   Drains the Hector and Garvie mountains and flows north-east to join the Kawarau River about 1 km downstream from the Victoria Bridge. It can be reached on the road from Bannockburn to Garston (Nevis–Cromwell road), but this is a very rough, dry-weather road most suited to four-wheel-drive vehicles.

Season   1 October–30 April.

Restrictions   Fly fishing only.

This river flows through dry, barren, inhospitable desert country, the scenery reminiscent of Western movie sets. The river doesn't hold great stocks of fish, but there are trophy trout present. A few years ago I met an elderly angler on the upper Ahuriri who had used a dry fly to take a brown trout from the Nevis that weighed in at 8 kg. He took an hour to land the fish, which now adorns his living room wall. The Nevis holds mainly browns, which can be spotted and stalked with dry flies or nymphs providing the downstream breeze is kind.

There's a very rough gorge in the lower reaches and the river is definitely boots-and-shorts territory. Use polaroids and practise relaxation before accurately casting to a fish, as the next fish may be a mile upstream if you put it down. It is best in December–January. The headwaters hold a wild stock of brook char (fontinalis), and the occasional rainbow adds to the enjoyment.

Mataura River tributaries in the Otago District

The Mataura River marks the boundary between the Otago and Southland Acclimatisation Societies' districts. See Southland District for the Mataura River and Southland tributaries. The season here lasts from 1 October to 30 April. The bag limit is 10 fish.

Waikaia River

Location and access   Like the Pomahaka River, the Waikaia rises in the Umbrella Mountains of Central Otago. It flows in a southerly direction for over 50 km to join the Mataura River at Riversdale. Access is possible from the Riversdale–Waikaia–Piano Flat roads.

This highly regarded brown trout fishery is the Mataura's major tributary. The inaccessible upper reaches above Piano Flat flow down a picturesque beech-clad valley but only hold a few fish. However, if one is prepared to tramp there are a few good, deep holes up as far as Whitecombe Flats 10 km or so upstream from Piano Flat (40 fish/km on drift dives at Piano Flat). The middle and lower reaches, with their willow-lined banks and shingle bed, wind across farmland. In clear, bright conditions, and despite the tea-stained water, fish can be spotted and fished for. But stocks are sufficiently great that 'blind' fly fishing can be just as rewarding.

There are long pools and runs, access is good and the river can be safely waded. It holds fish in the 0.75–1.5 kg range. A wide selection of flies will take fish, but try Dad's Favourite, Twilight Beauty, Blue Dun, Dark Red Spinner and Red Quill Gnat dry flies, Pheasant Tail, Hare's Ear and Half Back nymphs or Hardy's Favourite, March Brown, Purple Grouse and Twilight Beauty wet flies. At times a willow grub imitation can also be deadly.

Waikaka Stream

Location and access   Rises from the Black Umbrella Range and flows south, east of the Waikaia River, to enter the Mataura at Gore. Access is north of Gore at Willowbank, Maitland and Waikaka and from the Waikaka–Waikaia road.

This small stream holding small browns has been ruined by catchment works. Try the same methods as for the Waikaia, but spinning and live-bait fishing is also popular. The most enjoyable fly fishing water lies upstream from the township of Waikaka. There are a few good brown trout in this area and as the river has a relatively small catchment it can remain clear when other rivers in the district have become unfishable.

Mimihau Stream

Location and access   A small stream draining in a westerly direction to enter the Mataura River near Wyndham, just upstream of the Mokoreta River. Access to the middle and upper reaches is from the Waiarikiki–Mimihau road and the Waiarikiki road; to the lower reaches from the Wyndham–Mataura road.

Above Waiarikiki the river flows through patches of native bush and is a delight to fish. Fish can be spotted and stalked with small dry flies and nymphs. The rocky bed can be slippery for wading. Below Waiarikiki, the river tends to be discoloured and infested with willow, gorse and scrub, and it tends to get weedy in high summer, but there are areas where fishing is possible. Many fish are caught on live bait although the average size of fish taken from this stream is small.

Mokoreta River (Wyndham)

Location and access   Flows roughly parallel to, but south of, the Mimihau Stream to enter the Mataura below Wyndham. There is good road access from the Wyndham–Mokoreta–Clinton roads, often across private farmland.

The Wyndham Anglers' Club is very strong and members firmly believe that the rivers around Wyndham offer excellent brown trout fishing, so it pays to befriend a local angler! This stream offers good fishing for small fish early in the season before the river becomes low and choked with weed. The water is tea-stained, making spotting impossible, but there are sufficient fish to ensure successful blind fishing. The middle reaches are the most popular and brown trout can be taken on spinners, dry and wet flies, or using live bait.

Southland District

The Southland District includes the southernmost part of the South Island and Fiordland. In Southland there are four major river systems. The Mataura and Oreti rivers rise from mountainous bush and tussock-covered country south of Lake Wakatipu, while further west, the Waiau River drains Lakes Te Anau and Manapouri. The Aparima River, between the Waiau and Oreti rivers, rises in the Takitimu Mountains. All four rivers flow gently south across the fertile plains of Southland and empty into Foveaux Strait. Flooding is not uncommon in Southland; in 1984 a disastrous flood inundated the suburbs of Invercargill.

Most rivers hold brown trout introduced in 1870. Rainbow are only present in the Waiau River system and Lake Thomas. Occasionally, an Atlantic salmon is also caught in the Waiau. The township of Gore has laid claims to being the 'Trout Fishing Capital of New Zealand'. There's little doubt that Southland has some superb brown trout streams. The summer months are the best times to visit Southland when the weather is temperate and the prevailing westerly winds kind. There's a long twilight in the south and from December to the end of January it remains daylight until after 10 p.m.

Fiordland is a World Heritage Park. Land forms and climatic conditions vary enormously within this area. In the west, the region comprises precipitous bush-clad fiords and rugged mountains that are largely inaccessible. The annual rainfall can be as high as 6 800 mm (recorded at Dumpling Hut on the Milford Track). There's a wide variety of fishing water and even the isolated rivers can be reached from Te Anau or Queenstown by floatplane or helicopter. A number of airstrips in remote valleys, initially constructed for venison and deer recovery, can also be used. Tramping experience, accurate maps, and adequate equipment (including insect repellent) are essential for anglers venturing into Fiordland.

Nearly all moderate-sized rivers hold trout, but only those considered worthwhile will be described. Many rivers, and especially the headwaters, see no anglers for the whole season so the chances of catching a trophy fish in this remote region are high for those with the energy and tenacity to explore. Rivers can rise to terrifying levels in a very short time and just as quickly return to normal, so always allow for this by adding a few extra days when planning a trip into remote country. Never attempt a risky crossing when a river is rising.

Brown trout were first introduced into Lake Manapouri about 1875 and into the Lower Hollyford as early as 1884. Rainbow trout were released into Lake Te Anau in the mid-1920s; Atlantic salmon were released into Lake Ada in 1891 and into Lake Te Anau about 1910.

Unless otherwise stated the season opens on 1 October and closes on 30 April, and the bag limit is 10 trout or salmon.

Fiordland rivers and lakes

Awarua River

This river at the northern end of Big Bay draining the Waiuna Lagoon and swamp behind the sandhills offers excellent sea-run brown trout fishing during the whitebait season. I have seen trout actually surf in on the waves at the mouth while chasing whitebait. The river banks are overgrown and swampy. Though perhaps not worth visiting for trout fishing alone, for the tramper/angler, the trout here can provide great variety alongside whitebait, crayfish, blue-cod and paua!

Hollyford River

Location   Begins near the Homer Saddle on the Milford road and drains the Darren and Humboldt mountains. Flows north to enter the top end of Lake McKerrow then drains this lake by flowing into the sea at Martins Bay.

Access   Branch off the Milford road onto the Upper Hollyford road to Gunn's Camp. The road goes down the Hollyford Valley a short distance. From here one can either tramp or hire a jet boat. There's also an airstrip at Martins Bay. Flights can be arranged from Te Anau or Queenstown either by fixed-wing aircraft to Martins Bay or floatplane to Lake McKerrow.

Season   Open all year on the Hollyford and Pyke rivers.

Restrictions   The bag limit is 6 trout. Artificial bait only.

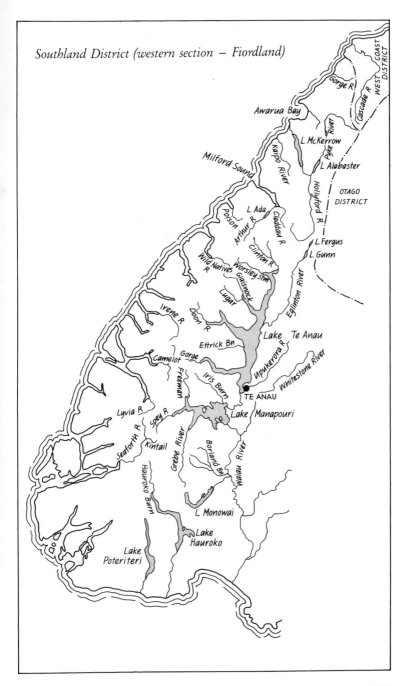

Southland District (western section – Fiordland)

WEST COAST DISTRICT

Gorge R.

Cascade R.

Awarua Bay

Pyke River

L McKerrow

Kaipo River

Milford Sound

L Alabaster

Hollyford R.

OTAGO DISTRICT

Poison

L Ada

Arthur R.

Cleddau R.

Clinton R.

L Fergus

L Gunn

Wild Natives R.

Worsley Stm

Glaisnock

Lugar

Eglinton River

Irene R.

Doon R.

Lake Te Anau

Ettrick Bn

Gorge

Camelot

Freeman

Iris Burn

Upukerora R.

Whitestone River

TE ANAU

Lyvia R.

Spey R.

Kintail

Grebe River

Borland Bn

Waiau River

Lake Manapouri

Seaforth R.

Hauroko Burn

L Monowai

Lake Hauroko

Lake Poteriteri

This wonderful, wild and scenic river holds brown trout up to 4.5 kg. The upper reaches are boisterous and rough but hold a few large fish in pocket water. Below Hidden Falls the valley flattens out and the river flows more sedately through runs and deep blue pools. Although the river is usually crystal clear, crossings are extremely hazardous and should only be attempted by the experienced during low water flows.

There's excellent fly fishing of all types and spin fishing from Gunn's Camp to Lake McKerrow. The 4–5 km of water from the outlet of Lake McKerrow to the mouth at Martins Bay is full of snags and is suitable for spinning only but holds good fish. Check the ranger station at Te Anau for accommodation at Hidden Falls, Alabaster, Demon Trail, Hokuri and Martins Bay huts.

Remember, this large river can rise alarmingly during heavy rain. I once spent four days at Martins Bay unable to cross a swollen creek that previously had been less than ankle deep. The Hidden Falls Creek itself usually holds a fish or two close to the hut, but floods may alter the pools from year to year. A few quinnat salmon from a release of smolt into the Pyke River have strayed into the lower reaches at Martins Bay over the past few years.

Lake McKerrow

Access Same as for the Hollyford Valley. Trampers need experience to enter this area, especially to tackle the Demon Trail along the eastern shore of the lake where windfalls can be a real problem with a heavy pack. Parks Board huts are available at the top of the lake and at Hokuri Creek.

Season Open all year.

Restrictions The bag limit is 6 fish.

This deep lake is over 20 km long and occupies an old drowned glacial valley. It is completely surrounded by steep, bush-clad hills. Although it is probably best suited to spin fishing there are parts of the shoreline where brown trout can be spotted cruising. A small, lightly weighted nymph in preference to a dry fly readily takes cruising fish. The Hollyford delta at the top end of the lake and the mouth of Hokuri Creek are hot spots for sunk lure fishing. Try Parson's Glory, Lord's and Hamill's Killer, Yellow Rabbit and Muddler Minnow.

Any black fly at night will catch fish; they are not very selective.

On one occasion when quietly stalking a fish near the outlet, my efforts were rudely interrupted by a school of dolphins entering the lake from Martins Bay. They swooped on the trout and then joyfully returned to the sea fully replenished.

Pyke River

Location and access   This tea-stained, sluggish, flood-prone river rises in the Red Hills, flows into and out of Lakes Wilmot and Alabaster and joins the Hollyford some 6 km upstream from its McKerrow mouth. Reached by tramping, helicopter or floatplane to Lake Alabaster.

The Pyke holds good brown trout upstream as far as the site of the old Pyke Hut behind Big Bay. Fish can usually be spotted but many logs in the river brought down by floods create an additional hazard for the angler playing a fish. There are healthy eels in most of the deep holes.

Lakes Wilmot and Alabaster

Location   Both these scenic bush-lined mountain lakes lie in the Pyke Valley.

Season   Open all year.

Restrictions   The bag limit is 6 fish.

Trout are difficult to spot unless the lakes are low, and fishing is generally best with a spinner. There are areas for the fly angler, such as the Pyke delta at the top end of both lakes where fish can be seen cruising in clear conditions. Late in the season spawning fish congregate in these areas and lure fishing with a Red Setter or Orange Rabbit is very productive. The scenery is superb, especially looking south from the top end of Lake Alabaster, the snow-covered Darren Mountains reflected in the lake presenting an unforgettable sight. There are browns up to 4.5 kg in these lakes and some large eels.

The Kaipo River enters the sea 10 km south of Martins Bay. There's a deer recovery airstrip on the top flats. Above these flats are a few stable pools overhung by beech bush holding large browns. Between the top flats and the gorge, the river is unstable and holds few fish.

Most stable water in the gorge holds fish and there is good estuarine spin fishing for sea-run browns. This information is generally of interest to tramper/anglers and hunters only.

Cleddau River

Location and access   Rises near the Homer Tunnel on the Milford Sound road (S.H.94) and has a short, steep course to Milford Sound.

Season   Open all year.

Restrictions   The bag limit is 6 fish.

The Cleddau holds good brown trout only in the lower reaches in the vicinity of the airstrip. Fish can be spotted beneath the swarms of sandflies and respond to dry flies and nymphs. I had great success between rain squalls with a size 16 home-made wingless dry fly tied with a barred rock hackle. Perhaps the trout imagined this contrivance to be a giant sandfly!

Action on the Borland Burn, above Lake Monowai.

Arthur River

Location and access   Rises near the McKinnon Pass and from the Sutherland Falls on the Milford Track and flows into and out of Lake Ada to enter Milford Sound near Sandfly Point. Access from the Milford Track. There's an airstrip at Quinton Hut.

Season   Open all year.

Restrictions   The bag limit is 6 fish.

This deep tea-stained bush river carries good-sized brown trout, but the high rainfall (in excess of 6 000 mm) and sandfly swarms deter most anglers. The river holds large volumes of water but is not easy to fish. Fish can readily be seen from the Milford Track, especially from the swingbridge at Boatshed Hut. I advise using a spinner.

Lake Ada also holds browns best fished with a spinner or from a boat. The shoreline is overgrown, swampy and very difficult. The lake is open all year and the bag limit is 6 fish.

Lake Te Anau and related waters

Lake Te Anau is open all year, while the season for rivers entering the lake opens on 1 November and closes on 31 May. The bag limit for Lake Te Anau is 6 fish.

Clinton River

Location and access   Rises near the McKinnon Pass on the Milford Track, flows south-east and enters the head of Lake Te Anau at Glade House. Access by boat from Te Anau Downs or Te Anau, or by tramping a very difficult route over Dore Pass from the Eglinton Valley. The Milford Track follows the river upstream. There's accommodation at Glade House or in the Parks Board huts, but arrangements must be made at the ranger station at Te Anau. Camping is permitted in the north branch only, not on the track, and again permission must be obtained.

Season   1 November–31 May.

Restrictions   The bag limit is 3 fish. Artificial bait only.

This is a magnificent river holding browns and rainbows up to 4 kg in gin-clear water. Fish are very shy, but a cautious approach, accurate casting and a long, fine trace so as not to line the fish will bring results. The river flows through heavy bush and is littered with sunken logs brought down in floods. (These act as wonderful hides for trout, as I found to my dismay on one occasion. I hooked a rainbow I'd guess weighed around 4 kg in superb condition on a Coch-y-bondhu dry fly. The fish turned and raced downstream at tremendous speed, disappearing under a great mass of driftwood and logs. I still dream of this fish rising to my fly, its great jaws smacking in the artificial.)

Fish can be taken on well-sunk nymphs and dry flies, but one or two fish a day is really good going. It only remains fine in this high rainfall area for three days on end, but the river seldom discolours. Insect repellent is essential.

Worsley Stream

Location and access   Drains Lakes Sumor and Brownlee, flows on an easterly course and enters the top end of Te Anau at Worsley Arm. Access by boat or floatplane.

Season   1 November–31 May.

Restrictions   The bag limit is 3 fish.

This remote and scenic river flows through rugged, bush-covered, mountainous terrain, the habitat of New Zealand wapiti herds, and holds browns and rainbows, the latter predominating. Fish up to 4 kg can be taken using similar fishing methods as for the Clinton. This is high quality fishing water, but the catch rate will not be high. There's a Parks Board hut near the mouth.

There are a number of clear mountain streams entering the western side of Lake Te Anau that are well worth fishing, with access by boat or floatplane. All drain steep, heavily bushed country, and anglers need to combine tramping with angling. Such streams are the Glaisnock River and the Lugar Burn, both entering the head of North Fiord, the Doon River entering the south-west arm of the Middle Fiord, and the Ettrick Burn entering the lake just north of the Te Ana-au Glowworm Caves.

Lakes Fergus and Gunn

Location and access   S.H.94, the Eglinton Valley road, skirts the shorelines of both lakes.

Season   1 October–31 May.

Restrictions   The bag limit is 6 fish.

Both these scenic lakes offer limited fishing owing to their heavily bushed shoreline, but both hold brown and rainbow trout and landlocked Atlantic salmon. This water is best fished from a boat, float tube or by threadlining from the shore. Recent (1988) releases of Atlantic salmon have been made in both lakes.

Eglinton River

Location and access   Flows into and out of Lakes Fergus and Gunn, then down the scenic Eglinton Valley, following a southerly direction, to enter Lake Te Anau north of Te Anau Downs. There is road access to the mouth from Te Anau Downs. S.H.94 follows the river upstream on its true left bank, although a walk across tussock flats and through beech bush is sometimes required to reach the river.

Season   1 November–31 May.

Restrictions   Fly fishing only. The bag limit is 3 fish.

This excellent river has easy access to clear water containing mainly rainbow but also a few brown trout. Fish can be spotted in clear, bright conditions and taken on dry flies, nymphs and sunk lures. There are well-defined pools and runs and the river can be crossed and waded in selected places at the tail of most pools. The riverbed is shingly and the banks covered with grass and patches of beech bush.

The lower and middle reaches around Walker Creek tend to hold most fish, though trout can be caught up as far as Cascade Creek. This is an important spawning river for Lake Te Anau. The east branch is unstable and not worth fishing. There are a few fish in the lower reaches of Smithy Creek flowing through the tussock just beyond Knobs Flat.

Upukeroro River

Location and access   Rises in the Livingstone Mountains and flows on a south-westerly course through farmland to enter Lake Te Anau at Patience Bay just north of Te Anau township. Access from S.H.94 3 km north of the township where the road crosses the river. Walk upstream from the bridge.

Season   1 November–31 May.

Restrictions   Fly fishing only. The bag limit is 3 fish.

An important spawning stream for Lake Te Anau, this river can dry somewhat during hot summer conditions. Upukeroro holds mainly browns with an odd rainbow, especially late in the season. Although close to Te Anau, there's a good population of fish in this river, wading is easy on a shingle bed and the pools and ripples are a delight to fish. Fish are easily seen and a bit scary but accept dry flies and nymphs carefully presented. Some fish I caught recently were a bit skinny. This river is ideal for the learner fly fisher, but catch and release is recommended.

Lake Te Anau

Season   Open all year.

Restrictions   The bag limit is 6 fish.

This is the largest lake in the South Island, being 61 km long and covering 850 ha. The western shore is broken up into fiords which penetrate deep into the rugged bush-covered Fiordland mountains. The eastern shore is drier, grass-covered and farmed. Te Anau township on the eastern shore is a tourist centre offering good accommodation and transport to various locations in Fiordland.

The lake is best fished by trolling from a boat or spinning from the shore though there are a few selected spots, mainly at stream mouths, where fly anglers can fish. Fish are hard to see except at shallow deltas such as the Eglinton, but they include rainbow and brown trout along with landlocked Atlantic salmon. The lake level is controlled at the outlet by a weir.

Upper Waiau River

> **Location and access**   Flows from Lake Te Anau to Lake Manapouri. Access off the Te Anau–Manapouri road and the Kepler Track from the Control Gates on Te Anau to Shallow Bay at Manapouri.
>
> **Season**   1 October–31 May.
>
> **Restrictions**   The bag limit is 6 fish.

This heavy, deep, clear water holds a good stock of brown and rainbow trout with an occasional Atlantic salmon. It's not easy to fish though unless using a threadline. Make sure your spinner sinks well down before retrieving. There are fly fishing spots at the Control Gates, Rainbow Reach and Balloon Loop. I have found the Kepler Track on the true right bank provides more scope if one is prepared to scramble down through bush to get to the river.

Downstream lure and upstream well-weighted nymph fishing is best during the day. At dusk, in favourable conditions, there is often a prolific evening rise just below the Control Gates. If a Twilight Beauty dry fly is unsuccessful, try a Purple Grouse, March Brown or Twilight Beauty wet fly on a floating line fished across the current. Fish take these flies as they begin to speed up on the swing and sport can be fast and furious. The lower 2 to 3 km are rather unstable, contain fallen trees and are unattractive to fish. The mouth at Manapouri is a favoured spot, but a boat is necessary for either spinning or deep lure fishing, as wading is treacherous in the soft sand.

Lake Manapouri

> **Season**   Open all year.
>
> **Restrictions**   The bag limit is 6 fish.

Manapouri is a beautiful, cold scenic lake surrounded by native bush. Regrettably it has been modified for power generation, and on my last visit, in 1989, the lake was very low with unattractive sand and mud banks exposed. The lake is very deep – at its maximum depth of 443 m it is 258 m below sea level.

I first visited this lake in 1945 as a 9-year-old and still possess a photograph of me proudly holding up two 2 kg Atlantic salmon caught trolling from Les Murrell's launch. The lake holds brown and rainbow trout, but the Atlantic salmon have not thrived and are rarely caught. Fish are very difficult to spot from the shore and trollers take 90 percent of the fish caught. Lure fishing at stream mouths, especially at night, is worth trying.

Iris Burn

Location and access   Rises in the Kepler Mountains and flows south-west to enter Lake Manapouri 3 km west of Shallow Bay. Access from the Kepler Track.

Season   1 November–31 May.

Restrictions   The bag limit is 3 fish.

The lower reaches are unstable and flood-prone. There are a few fish below the Big Slip, and fishing is only worthwhile above this point. A shallow, swampy lake has been formed by the lake and this holds rainbow trout in the 0.75–1.5 kg range. The river above the slip holds a few fish but they are not in good condition. The predominant fish here is rainbow. The Iris Burn is only worth visiting as a diversion from walking the Kepler Track.

The Forest Burn is also reputed to hold fish, but it was in flood when I visited. The Freeman Burn entering the North Arm also holds trout and is similar to the Iris Burn.

Spey River

Location and access   Rises near Centre Pass on the Manapouri–Dusky Sound Track, flows north-east and enters the lake at West Arm. Access by boat to West Arm and then from the road to Doubtful Sound.

Season   1 November–31 May.

Restrictions   The bag limit is 3 fish.

Fishing has deteriorated since the Manapouri power scheme and the road to Doubtful Sound were built, but beyond the road end there

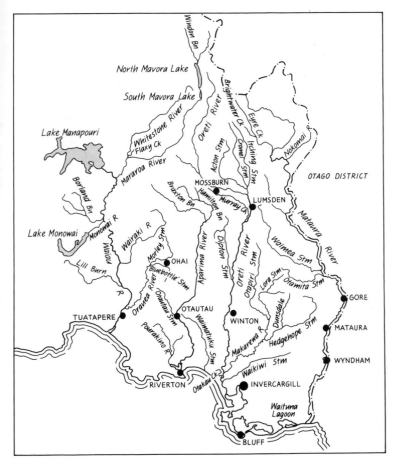

Southland District (eastern section)

is still reasonable fly fishing for rainbows in clear mountain water. The track over Centre Pass to Dusky Sound follows up the true left bank.

Grebe River

Location and access   Flows north to enter the South Arm of Manapouri. Access by boat to South Arm or by the metalled hydro road from Monowai that has been recently opened to the public. This leaves Borland Lodge, crosses a saddle and descends into the

Grebe Valley to follow up the true left bank. It is rough and unsuitable for trailers.

Season   1 November–31 May.

Restrictions   The bag limit is 3 fish.

The Grebe is a similar river to the Spey and holds brown and rainbow trout. The fishing has not improved since the hydro road from Monowai was built, but the valley is still worth visiting if you ignore the power pylons. Just over the saddle, before the road reaches the Grebe River, there are two small tarns. The one furthest from the road, on the left, holds large brown trout.

Home Creek

Location and access   Drains swampy land north-east of Manapouri and empties into the Waiau River downstream from Manapouri. Access across private farmland 3 km from Manapouri on the Hillside–Manapouri road. Permission required.

Season   1 October–31 May.

Restrictions   The bag limit is 3 fish.

This small, clear creek lined with scrub and flax holds a reasonable head of fish that really test an angler's ability. Fish fine with small dry flies and weighted nymphs on a long trace. Fish can be seen.

Lake Monowai

Location and access   Lies south of Manapouri and north-west of Tuatapere. Access to Monowai from the Blackmount–Clifden road.

Season   Open all year.

Restrictions   The bag limit is 6 fish.

The lake, 22 km long and surrounded by bush, has been modified for power generation; as a consequence of raising the level, it now presents a grotesque appearance with tree stumps protruding above water level in certain areas.

Shoreline fishing is very limited, but there's good trolling in the lake for browns and rainbows averaging more than 2 kg. The mouth of the Electric River at June Bay and the Roger Inlet are favoured locations. Boat-launching facilities are sited near the outlet. For the adventurous angler, the Electric River is worth exploring but is very overgrown by native bush. (See Waiau tributaries for the Monowai River and Borland Burn.)

Lake Hauroko

Location and access   Lies south of Monowai and west of Clifden and Tuatapere. Road access from S.H.96 at Clifden on the Lillburn Valley road. There's a Parks Board shelter at the lake and a concrete boat ramp at the road end.

Season   Open all year.

Restrictions   The bag limit is 6 fish.

A larger lake than Monowai, and very exposed to strong nor'west winds which whistle down the lake, Hauroko is best fished by trolling from a boat as the lake is surrounded by dense bush. Both the bay at the road end and the bay at the signposted picnic area are shallow. Cruising brown trout can be stalked in these areas despite the light tea-coloured water.

The Hauroko Burn entering the head of the lake offers good fishing for those walking to Dusky Sound.

Lake Poteriteri

Season   Open all year.

Restrictions   The bag limit is 6 fish.

This long, remote, bush-surrounded lake lies south-west of Lake Hauroko, and is very difficult to reach except by floatplane or by tramping the southern coast from Port Craig and then following up the Waitutu River to the lake. But it does hold brown trout, most of which would never have seen an angler. There's a Fiordland National Parks Board hut on the eastern shore.

Isolated rivers and lakes of Fiordland

Information is very sketchy on many of the rivers entering the Tasman Sea south of Milford Sound. However, though I have only visited a few of these rivers I can confirm that many of the larger waterways hold trout. Access is very difficult through this rugged inhospitable mountain country, where the annual rainfall is around 6 000 mm and the prevailing strong westerly winds, sandflies and mosquistoes deter all but the hardiest of anglers.

Access is by helicopter or floatplane from Te Anau or fishing boat from Milford or Bluff. February and March are the most settled months to visit these rivers. The following hold brown trout:

Transit River entering the Tasman Sea at Transit Beach, immediately south of Milford Sound.

Poison River at Poison Bay, also south of Milford Sound.

Light and Dark (lower) rivers entering Sutherland Sound.

Wild Natives River at the head of Bligh Sound.

George River entering George Sound.

Edith River draining into Lake Alice at George Sound.

Stillwater River draining into Lake Marchant at Caswell Sound.

Large Burn joining Lakes Mackinnon and Marchant.

Irene and Windward rivers entering Charles Sound.

Camelot River at the head of Bradshaw Sound. There are two lagoons on this river formed by landslides below the Bedivere Falls and these contain large brown trout.

Seaforth River and Kintail Burn. Quinnat salmon were released into the Seaforth River in 1911 and salmon carcasses were reported as recently as 1971. There is no up-to-date information on salmon, but the rivers certainly hold brown trout and there's excellent fishing in the Kintail Burn on the Manapouri–Dusky Sound Track.

Long Burn draining into Lake Widgeon at Long Sound.

Waitutu River draining Lake Poteriteri. Access by tramping the southern Fiordland coastline from Port Craig.

Green Lake lies just north of Lake Monowai. There's a tramping track to this lake from the Lake Monowai outlet.

Lake Hakapoua. This extremely isolated lake lies just inland from the southern coast of Fiordland. Access by tramping the coastline from Port Craig beyond the Waitutu River to the Big River.

The following hold brown and rainbow trout:

Lyvia River at Deep Cove, Doubtful Sound, and the tailrace emptying into Doubtful Sound from the hydro-electric power scheme at West Arm, Manapouri, both hold rainbow and brown trout. The rainbow have somehow come through the powerhouse and survived. Fish from the tailrace have spread into the neighbouring Lyvia River. It is overgrown with bush and not easy to fish, however. There's access to both the tailrace and the Lyvia River from the road linking the West Arm to Doubtful Sound. *Lakes Thomson and Hankinson* beyond the North-west Arm of the Middle Fiord of Lake Te Anau.

If you are brave or foolish enough to venture into these areas specifically to fish you certainly deserve the best of luck!

Waiau River and tributaries

Waiau River (below the Mararoa weir)

Location This large river drained Lake Manapouri before the weir was built below the Mararoa confluence; now this water is redirected back into the lake for hydro-electricity generation at West Arm. Below the weir the river follows a southerly course near Monowai and Clifden to eventually reach Te Waewae Lagoon south of Tuatapere.

Access Roads generally don't follow close to the river, though S.H.96 crosses the lower reaches at Clifden and Tuatapere. Some areas of the river are difficult to reach because of scrub and bush on the banks, but there is access from a road leaving the top of the Redcliff Saddle, from Monowai, and south of Monowai through private land at Sunnyside Station; also from Glendearg Station (road off S.H.96 north of Clifden) and Motu Bush Road off the Lillburn Valley road.

Season Below the Mararoa weir, 1 October–30 April. The tidal section near the mouth is open all year.

Restrictions Downstream from the weir the bag limit is 10 fish.

Although this river has been severely modified and reduced in size and volume it still provides good fishing for brown and rainbow trout. Wading can be hazardous on the algae-covered stones, and when the water is allowed to spill over the weir to clear the silt the river runs discoloured for some time. Fish cannot generally be spotted. The lower reaches and mouth are often fished with live bait and spinners for sea-run or estuarine-living browns, especially during October and again in April. After the end of November there's reasonable dry fly fishing, especially in the upper reaches below the weir. Some large fish have been taken from this river, including, a few years ago, a brown trout weighing 13.9 kg.

Whitestone River

Location and access   Rises from the Livingstone Mountains to the west of Mavora Lakes, flows on a southerly course and joins the lower reaches of the Mararoa River south of the Manapouri road in the Mt York area. Access from the Hillside–Manapouri road to the lower reaches, S.H.94 (the Lumsden–Te Anau road) to the middle reaches and Kakapo Road, off S.H.94, to the upper reaches.

Season   1 October–30 April.

Restrictions   The bag limit is 4 fish.

This small stream draining the Snowden State Forest and flowing through pastoral land tends to dry in summer, though there are still some good pools in the upper reaches that can be fished even when the river is very low at the S.H.94 bridge. It holds small numbers of large browns and rainbows which can be stalked but in clear, low-water conditions present a real challenge. Catch and release is strongly recommended.

Mararoa River

Location and access   Rises between the Livingstone and Thomson mountains just south of Greenstone Valley, flows south down a barren tussock valley and into North Mavora Lake. Drains this lake and enters the bush-clad South Mavora Lake 4 km further south. Emerges from South Mavora and continues through bush for 3 km before the valley opens out into tussock and farmland. The river becomes braided in this section, then flows south for over 40 km before joining the Whitestone River south of the Hillside–Manapouri road. After flowing through a gorge the river joins the Waiau 6.5 km south of Lake Manapouri.

Season   1 October–30 April.

Restrictions   The bag limit is 4 fish.

Upper reaches

Access   The top end of North Mavora Lake can be reached by four-wheel-drive only on a rough track along the eastern side of the lake. Between the two lakes and downstream from the South Mavora outlet there is access off the Te Anau–Mavora Lakes road.

The Upper Mararoa River runs through a very exposed tussock valley but holds a few large fish in the first 1–2 km above North Mavora Lake. These must be approached with care. The Windon Burn entering the Mararoa from the west also holds a few good fish in the lower pools, especially early and late in the season. There are usually a few fish between the two lakes, where the water is deep, clear and fast-flowing.

At the southern end of South Mavora Lake the river is stable for 3 km and flows through bush and tussock on a rock and stone bed. This superb river holds mainly brown trout in the 1.2–3 kg range (25 large fish/km on drift dives). There are a few rainbow below South Mavora Lake and downstream from S.H.94. Don't be fooled by first impressions, as although much of the water downstream from the bush is braided and looks unstable it holds good stocks of fish, which can be spotted. The river can be crossed below most pools, but the stones are very slippery.

The water remains fishable after rain, but the catch rate falls off when the river runs high. Try Deer Hair, Mole Fly and Palmer variety dry flies in the rough water in sizes 8–12, Twilight Beauty, Dad's Favourite, Greenwell's Glory and Coch-y-bondhu in sizes 12–16 in the calmer stretches, March Brown and Twilight Beauty wet flies and Mrs Simpson and Muddler Minnow lures. Any well-weighted nymph will take fish in the rough water, but use smaller sizes in the pools.

Middle reaches

Access   S.H.94 crosses the river just beyond The Key. Turn off S.H.94 at Burwood Station onto the Te Anau–Mavora Lakes road, which leads upstream on the true left bank to South Mavora Lake. The Centre Hill–Mavora Lakes road, also off S.H.94, joins this road at the apex of a triangle.

There's good water downstream from the main roadbridge on S.H.94 and upstream off the Te Anau–Mavora Lakes road. Although these stretches appear rather unstable and shingly, there is excellent fly fishing in the runs and pools. Fish can be spotted, but the nor'wester can be a problem for the upstream fly angler.

Lower reaches

> **Access**   Weir Road from Manapouri follows down the Waiau River and crosses the Mararoa River below its gorge and near the weir.

There's reasonable fishing above this bridge and upstream through the gorge for the active boots-and-shorts angler. Higher upstream, after the Hillside–Manapouri roadbridge over the Whitestone River, look for a track on the left 1.5 km further down the road towards Manapouri. This leads downstream to the Whitestone confluence, Flaxy Creek and the top end of the gorge. There are usually a few fish in the lower reaches of Flaxy Creek.

Borland Burn

> **Location and access**   Rises in the Hunter Mountains and flows south-east through native bush to enter the Waiau 1.6 km above Monowai power station. Access off the Monowai road to Borland Lodge and then by a marked track to North Borland Hut. It's a 15-minute walk through the bush to the river. The first stream crossed is the deeply tea-coloured Pig Creek.
>
> **Season**   1 October–30 April.
>
> **Restrictions**   The bag limit is 4 fish.

This clear wadable rock and stone stream flowing through bush holds good-sized browns and rainbows that are shy but easily spotted in the pools and runs. This river is highly recommended for the skilful boots-and-shorts fly angler carrying sandfly repellent and not worried about hooking trees on the backcast. It floods readily but clears rapidly.

Monowai River

> **Location and access**   The Lake Monowai road crosses this river 1 km past Monowai Village and parallels the river on its true left bank to the lake outlet. There are three or four four-wheel-drive access tracks through the manuka scrub to the river off this road.
>
> **Restrictions**   The bag limit is 4 fish.

A moderately fast-flowing, overgrown, gin-clear river, the Monowai is difficult to fish but holds excellent brown trout averaging close to 2 kg. In parts the river is deep and slow-flowing over a stone and weed bed, but there are also some fast runs. It remains clear even after heavy rain. Steeple and roll casts are required from anglers using a fly rod as the river is difficult to wade. It is much easier to threadline. Fish are selective and shy but well worth the effort. The stream level fluctuates according to power requirements and there's only 6 km of river to fish above the power station intake. Well-weighted Hare and Copper nymphs are worth trying in the runs, but much lighter gear is necessary in the slower-flowing sections. The sandflies and mosquitoes are voracious!

Wairaki River

Location and access   Rises in the Takitimu Mountains, flows south-west and enters the Waiau 10 km north of Clifden. The Clifden–Blackmount road crosses the lower reaches.

Season   1 October–30 April.

Restrictions   The bag limit is 4 fish. Artificial bait only above the transmission lines.

This small, unstable, shingly river is prone to flooding and holds minimal stocks of fish. The upper reaches, with four-wheel-drive access through private land on Mt Linton Station, offer more stable water.

Lill Burn

Location and access   Drains the Kaherekoau Mountains north-east of Lake Hauroko and follows a north-easterly course to join the Waiau 5 km north of Clifden. The Lillburn Valley road to Lake Hauroko follows the river upstream and provides easy access across farmland.

Season   1 October–30 April.

Restrictions   The bag limit is 4 fish.

A medium-sized, tea-coloured stream emerging from native bush and flowing gently across pasture land, Lill Burn is choked with willows in parts but holds a good stock of brown trout in the 1–2 kg range, especially in the lower 10 km of river. Fish numbers decrease in the bush-lined section.

With a sand and shingle bed, this is a very pleasant river to fish and is recommended as a fly stream. Fish can be spotted and rise freely even during the heat of the day. The best fish are naturally found in the willow-choked stretches.

Orauea River (Orawia)

Location and access   Three small streams, the Sharpridge, Morley and Bluebottle, rise from country surrounding Ohai and join to form the Orauea near Birchwood. The main river then flows across pastoral farmland to enter the Waiau just upstream from Tuatapere. The Otautau–Tuatapere road and S.H.96 from Orawia to Ohai follow the river. Sharpridge Creek can be approached from Birchwood on S.H.96, Morley Stream from Mt Linton Road, north of Birchwood, and Bluebottle Stream from Bluebottle Road, south from Ohai.

Season   1 October–30 April.

Restrictions   The bag limit is 4 fish.

The tea-coloured Lill Burn flowing through native bush and willows.

The main river is choked with willows in parts but holds a reasonable stock of brown trout in the 0.75–1.2 kg range. For the fly angler, the best water in the main river lies upstream of Pukemaori. The lower Morley and the Orauea have in the past been polluted by coal-mine effluent from Ohai but have recently improved. In low-water summer conditions, weed growth is a problem from farm drainage. The Bluebottle appears slow-flowing and uninteresting, but put a dry fly on some of the deeper, still pools and let it sit there; the results can be surprising. The Sharpridge is a small stream but holds quite large fish, which rise to dry flies such as Mole Fly and Pevril o' the Peak in sizes 8–10. Fish can also be taken on spinners and live bait though the tributaries should be reserved for fly only.

Mavora Lakes

Location and access   Lie between the Livingstone and Thomson mountains just south and west of Lake Wakatipu. From S.H.94 take the branch roads to Mavora Lakes from either Centre Hill or Burwood Station. These roads join and follow up the Mararoa River to the lakes.

Season   1 October–30 April.

Restrictions   Artificial bait only. The bag limit is 4 trout.

North Mavora is 9.5 km long and, except for patches of beech bush near the southern end, is surrounded by tussock- and matagouri-covered mountains. There's a rough four-wheel-drive track up the east side of the lake to the head. Brown trout can be spotted cruising the lake margins and will accept dry flies, nymphs and small lures. The lake has deteriorated as a fishery since the road was built 20 years ago and boats introduced, but fish still average 1.6 kg.

In 1958 I tramped in from the Greenstone Valley over the Mararoa Saddle, and I still possess a photo of a 4 kg brown caught round the lake edge on a dry fly. Large herds of fallow deer roamed the Upper Mararoa Valley in those days.

South Mavora is smaller – a mere 2.5 km long – and is more sheltered, with a mainly bush-covered shoreline. There's good fly fishing for cruising trout round the lake margin and in the shallow inlets, especially at the northern end where the river enters. Fish are also taken on spinners and by trolling. However, the peaceful tranquillity of a high-country lake is now often disturbed during summer by powerboats, water-skiers and trail bikes. Camping sites with minimal facilities are available. The lakes are worth visiting for their scenic beauty alone. Try the same flies as listed for the Mararoa River.

Note: The Upper Oreti River is close by and well worth visiting.

Lake Thomas

Location and access   Lies 4 km from Mararoa Station north of The Key. Turn off S.H.94 2.5 km on the Te Anau side of the Mararoa Bridge. Lagoon Creek Road and Danby Road lead to the lake.

Restrictions   No boats allowed. The bag limit is 4 fish.

This small, shallow, exposed lake covers 10 ha and holds good-sized rainbows. Lagoon Creek drains into the Mararoa River.

Aparima River and tributaries

Aparima River (Jacobs)

Location and access   Rises in the Takitimu Mountains. The headwaters flow east, but after being joined by the Hamilton and Braxton burns south of Mossburn the river turns to flow south across farmland and eventually reaches the sea at the Jacobs River estuary at Riverton. Roads follow both banks of this river and there are anglers' access tracks. The upper reaches (Jacobs River) can be reached on the Dunrobin Valley road through private land on Dunrobin Station. A four-wheel-drive vehicle is an advantage in this area.

Restrictions   Upstream from the Otautau–Mossburn highway (Jacobs Bridge) the bag limit is 4 fish and artificial bait only may be used. Below Gummies Bush roadbridge the river is open all year round except during May and the bag limit is 10 fish.

The Aparima holds good stocks of brown trout in the 0.75–1.5 kg range and offers fly fishing in the middle and upper reaches, spinning in the middle and lower reaches, and live-bait fishing, especially in the lower tidal section. The river is willow-lined and flows over a shingle bed offering good, safe wading in most stretches. There are long, wide glides and shallow, shingly riffles.

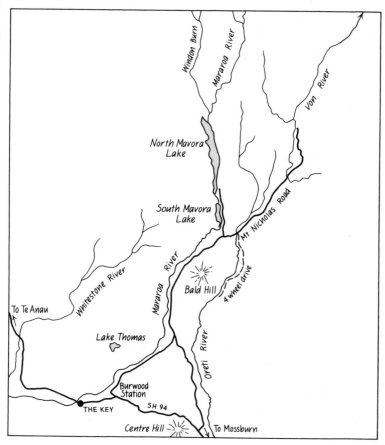

Mavora Lakes

The fly angler is advised to fish upstream above Wreys Bush. (Drift dives have registered 130 fish/km above Otautau, 50 percent of these being medium-sized fish.) Fish are not easy to spot except in the upper reaches, where the river tends to be more boisterous and bouldery, but the high density of fish means good sport can be had fishing 'blind'. There are some large sea-run fish in the lower reaches, especially early in the season. Beware the nor'wester, as this wind creates impossible conditions for upstream fishing; a gentle sou'wester is ideal.

A wide selection of flies will take fish, but I suggest you try Twilight Beauty, Dad's Favourite, Red Tipped Governor and Coch-y-bondhu dry flies in sizes 12–18, and March Brown, Purple Grouse, Waipihi

Red and Twilight Beauty wet flies. Old favourites Pheasant Tail and Hare's Ear weighted nymphs are always effective, especially in the smaller sizes, and a willow grub imitation can also be deadly at times. Fish become very shy in low-water summer conditions.

Hamilton Burn

Location and access   The North and South Braxton burns, the Braxton Burn itself, Hamilton Burn and Centre Burn all rise in the northern Takitimu Mountains and join before entering the Aparima 15 km south of Mossburn. Access from the Otautau–Mossburn highway, the Dipton–Mossburn road, Goodall Road, Waterloo Road and Mt Hamilton Road to the upper reaches.

Restrictions   The bag limit is 4 fish. Artificial bait only above the Otautau–Mossburn highway.

Both the Hamilton and Braxton burns (especially the north branch) offer classical small stream dry fly and nymph water for good-sized brown trout, especially in the middle and upper reaches. Fish can be spotted but are very shy and wary. The banks are lined with willow, broom gorse and flax, and as much of the water is weedy, slow-flowing and clear, good skills are needed for success. Fine tippets and small flies seem most effective. The nor'wester can 'kill' the stream. I recently met an angler using a No. 4 weight-forward floating line, 1.5 kg tapered nylon and size 18–20 dry flies on this stream. Luckily, the nor'wester was not blowing! Use the same flies as listed for the Aparima, only a size or two smaller.

Pourakino River

Location and access   Rises from the forested Longwood Range west of Riverton, follows a south-easterly course and enters the Jacobs (Aparima) River estuary at Riverton.

Season   Below the Pourakino Valley bridge the river is open all year except during May.

The Pourakino holds good sea-run browns, but these are best fished for by boat either by trolling or spinning. The river is generally slow-flowing, though there is a limited section of fly water in the upper reaches from the end of Pourakino Valley Road and Ermedale Road, where the river flows through thick beech bush.

Waimatuku Stream

Location and access   Rises from springs and swampland east of Otautau, and flows south across farmland to enter the sea south of Waimatuku. Access from Hamilton's bridge at the mouth, Waimatuku on S.H.99 and from roads in the region of Waimatuku, Otahuti and Isla Bank. Try Fraser Road, the Isla Bank–Flints Bush road and Isla Bank Road.

A highly regarded dry fly stream in the middle reaches, where access is good across private farmland, this stream has grassy banks, is fordable and is very pleasant to fish. It is best fished early in the season as weed growth in summer from farm run-off becomes a problem. Fish rise enthusiastically even during the day. The tidal section below Hamilton's bridge yields good sea-run browns to spinners early in the season.

Oreti River and tributaries
Oreti River

Location and access   Rises in the Thomson Mountains just east of North Mavora Lake and flows south for over 130 km before entering the New River estuary at Invercargill.

Restrictions   Above Mossburn (Rocky Point is signposted) the bag limit is 4 fish and artificial bait only is permitted. Below Rocky Point the bag limit is 10 fish. The tidal section is open all year except during May.

For convenience, the river is divided into four sections.

Upper reaches (above Mossburn)

Access   S.H.94 follows the river from Mossburn to the Mavora Lakes turn-off. The Centre Hill–Mavora Lakes road then follows the river upstream but leaves it when it passes on the west side of Bald Hill. Mt Nicholas Road crosses the upper Oreti 2 km after leaving the Mavora Lakes road (see Mavora Lakes map).

Downstream from the upper Oreti bridge on Mt Nicholas Road there is good fly fishing for a few large fish. Access is restricted by a locked gate so a good deal of walking is necessary. Fish stocks are not high (2–3 fish/km), so large stretches of water need to be covered. The river, which has a shingle bed, winds across exposed tussock flats.

Trout can be spotted and stalked, but the prevailing nor'wester can handicap the upstream fly angler. Trophy fish can be caught in this section, but the fish are shy and sophisticated and will only be deceived by expert fly presentation. When frightened, they dive for cover under the tussock banks. Try Palmer and Deer Hair varieties, Mole Fly, Coch-y-bondhu and Royal Wulff dry flies in sizes 10–12 or moderately weighted size 14 Pheasant Tail nymphs.

If the wind prevents upstream fishing, try floating a nymph on a long trace down with the current to fish you can see — it's helpful to have a mate spotting for you when using this technique. If this fails, a Muddler Minnow swung across the current on a slow-sinking line may very occasionally prove successful. Just above Mossburn, 60 fish/km have been counted on drift dives, half of these good-sized fish.

Middle reaches (Mossburn to Centre Bush)

Access   Between Mossburn and Lumsden from S.H.94 and between Lumsden and Centre Bush from S.H.6.

The river in this section is occasionally willow-lined though more often the banks are open and exposed. It flows over an unstable shingle bed, but there are good long glides and riffles. Fish are difficult to spot so fish blind with Dad's Favourite, Coch-y-bondhu or Twilight Beauty dry flies, Pheasant Tail and Olive nymphs or March Brown wet flies, all in the smaller sizes.

Lower reaches (from Centre Bush bridge to the Invercargill-Riverton (S.H.99) roadbridge)

Below Winton the river is slower-flowing and willow-lined with mud banks, and spinning and live-bait fishing become more effective, although fish can still be taken on flies. It holds good stocks of smaller fish in the 0.5–1 kg range.

Tidal section (below the S.H.99 bridge)

Season   Open all year round except May.

This stretch is quite heavily fished from boats and from the shore. The mouth of the Waikiwi Stream is a hot spot; methods used including live bait, spinning, smelt fly fishing and trolling. Trophy sea-run or estuarine-living fish are not uncommon, and only a few years ago a brown trout weighing 11.25 kg was caught on a worm in this section at the end of September. Fishing is best from half tide to low water in a westerly wind.

Irthing, Cromel and Acton Streams

Location and access   All three streams drain the Eyre Mountains north of Mossburn and join near Lowther just west of S.H.6 and 2 km upstream from the Ellis Road bridge. Access is from the Mossburn–Five Rivers road, Ellis, Irthing, Lowther and Selby roads and across private farmland.

Season   1 October–30 April.

Restrictions   The bag limit is 4 fish.

All these small, shingly, willow-lined streams winding across farmland hold browns averaging 1 kg. Occasionally a large fish up to 4 kg is caught, especially in the headwaters. The streams are a delight to fish, with grassy banks, pools and runs, but they tend to dry in summer, and farming operations have not improved the water quality. The Irthing tends to hold most water in summer and hence is favoured above the others. Drift dives in the Irthing reveal 150 trout/km, but most are small.

Murray Creek, at Josephville, Stag Stream, at Caroline, and Dipton Stream, at Dipton West, all join the west bank of the Oreti. All hold limited stocks of small brown trout but are not easy to fish because of flax and other streamside vegetation. They are important spawning streams.

Makarewa River

Location and access   This river, along with several other headwater tributaries – the Otapiri, Lora, Dunsdale, Hedgehope and Te Tipua – rises in the Hokonui Hills. The main river is rather sluggish and meanders slowly across the Southland Plain in a southerly direction to enter the Oreti River 11 km upstream from Invercargill.

Access is from numerous roads in the vicinity of Wallacetown, Makarewa Junction, Tussock Creek and Hokonui.

Season   Open all year except for May downstream from S.H.99 bridge at Wallacetown. Elsewhere, 1 October–30 April.

Restrictions   The bag limit is 10 trout.

The Makarewa is mainly fished with live bait and spinners. Freezing works pollution has lessened, but the river easily becomes eutrophic in summer with weed growth causing major angling problems.

Otapiri Stream

Location and access   Flows south through the Otapiri Gorge, then across farmland to join the Makarewa just north of Hedgehope. Take roads north and west of Hokonui and the Otapiri Gorge road.

Season   1 October–30 April.

Restrictions   The bag limit is 4 trout.

The lower reaches have been modified for flood control and are not worth fishing. The middle and upper reaches, especially through the Gorge, offer excellent dry fly water with fish in the 0.75–1 kg range. The banks feature grass, scrub and willow and the riverbed is gravel. Wading and crossing is easy and fish can be spotted and stalked with fine gear. Some slow-flowing pools will really test the angler.

This stream is best fished early and late in the season when flow rates are reasonable. Try Dad's Favourite, Red Quill Gnat, Twilight Beauty, Greenwell's Dark and Coch-y-bondhu dry flies in sizes 14–18. A Corixa (waterboatman) or midge pupa imitation is often useful for these selective fish, as are lightly weighted nymphs in the smaller sizes. There are good picnic sites in the Gorge.

Lora Stream

Location and access   Joins the Makarewa at Lora School just north of Hokonui. Access from the Lora River and Lora Gorge roads.

The Lora is a small accessible dry fly stream with a shingle bed. It holds small brown trout and is best fished in the middle and upper reaches early and late in the season, before water flows are reduced.

Hedgehope Stream

This stream joins the Makarewa at Tussock Creek bridge. Access is off Hedgehope Road south of Hedgehope and S.H.96 west of Glencoe. It holds small browns but has been ruined by channelling and is not highly recommended.

Dunsdale Stream

Location and access   Joins the Hedgehope Stream south of Hedgehope. Access from Dunsdale Valley Road east of Hedgehope off S.H.96.

A small fly stream with a rock and stone bed and banks of willow gorse and scrub, the Dunsdale holds small browns, but there's a limited amount of water to fish. Great picnic spots though.

Lake Waituna

This rather unattractive exposed tidal lagoon lies on the south coast at Toestoes Bay some 25 km east of Invercargill. Access south of Kapuka is off S.H.92 on Kapuka South Road and Waituna Lagoon Road. The lagoon offers boat fishing, live-bait fishing, spinning and smelt fly fishing for sea-run browns from October to December. The outlet is the hot spot.

Stalking big browns in the Upper Oreti River.

Mataura River and tributaries

The Mataura River marks the boundary between the Otago and Southland districts. Some tributaries of the Mataura, namely the Waikaia, Waikaka, Mimihau and Mokoreta rivers, have been described under the Otago District.

Mataura River

> **Location and access**   Rises from the Eyre and Garvie mountains south of Lake Wakatipu. Follows a south-easterly course to Gore, where it turns and flows south to finally empty into Toestoes Bay at Fortrose.
>
> **Season**   Below the Gorge Road traffic bridge on S.H.92 the river is open all year except for the month of May. Elsewhere, 1 October–30 April.
>
> **Restrictions**   The bag limit upstream from the Black bridge at Athol is 4 fish; elsewhere, 10 fish.

This famous brown trout river provides about 150 km of easy fishable water. For convenience, the river is here divided into three sections.

Upper Mataura (Fairlight to Cattle Flat)

> **Access**   Access above Garston from S.H.6 is across private farmland and permission must be obtained. There are fish upstream as far as Fairlight. Between Garston and Athol the river is small and willow-lined and flows over farmland. Access is not a problem, but again ask permission before crossing private land. Below Parawa, a shingle road running east gives good access to the Nokomai Gorge.

There are reasonable stocks of brown trout in the 0.75–1.2 kg range, which can be spotted under bright, low-water conditions in summer. However, the water is a greenish-grey colour and fish are difficult to see when the river runs above normal. There's miles of good fishing water, even right down through the Nokomai Gorge (40 fish/km at Nokomai on drift dives with 40 percent a good size), and the river is easily crossed at the tail of most pools, though the stones tend to be slippery.

One of the features of the Mataura River is that even in cold conditions in early spring there's often a good rise. Mayflies and caddis form the bulk of the trouts' diet, so try Dad's Favourite, Twilight Beauty, Kakahi Queen, Dark Red Spinner and Blue Dun dry flies in sizes 14–18. Sunk Pheasant Tail and Hare's Ear nymphs will often take fish, as will March Brown, Purple Grouse and Twilight Beauty wet flies.

In warm summer evenings when fish are rising vigorously try a caddis imitation or a sparsely tied wet fly fished sensitively upstream or across and down on a floating line. Even a Hairy Dog, Fuzzy Wuzzy or Mrs Simpson fished deep through the pools after dark can be rewarding. If the river is high and discoloured, try spinning with an Articulated Trout, Veltic or Devon.

Middle reaches (Cattle Flat down to Gore)

> **Access** There are many good access points, including from the Ardlussa–Cattle Flat road, Ardlussa bridge, Waipounamu bridge, Pyramid bridge at Riversdale, Mandeville, Otamita bridge, Monaghans Beach at Croydon and Graham's Island at Gore.

This is the most popular stretch of river, where it is slower-flowing and grass and willow-lined and meanders across farmland. It becomes a large river below the Waikaia confluence after which fording is hazardous. Fish are difficult to spot unless rising or cruising the backwaters, but stocks are high, especially below the Waikaia. Use the same methods as outlined for the Upper Mataura with the addition of willow grub imitations in December and January.

Lower Mataura (Gore to the mouth)

> **Access** There's good road access to many well-known fishing spots on the Lower Mataura.

The river is larger and deeper here and water quality deteriorates, especially below Mataura Island. Fish cannot be spotted, but they are prolific. At times the 'mad Mataura rise' can be totally frustrating. Use the same flies and methods as described above, but a small, lightly weighted dark nymph fished upstream can bring results when all else fails. Below Mataura Island the river becomes less attractive but still provides good fishing, especially in the stretch from Wyndham down to Gorge Road bridge on S.H.92 at the top of the tidal section. Live-bait methods are popular in this stretch.

Brightwater Stream

This small, clear, weedy, spring-fed stream flows across private farmland just south of Fairlight. Please ask permission from the landowner before fishing. Use the same flies as for the Mataura, but as the fish are a good size and very shy, a careful approach is essential. This is an important spawning stream but, being spring-fed, it does not colour during a fresh. Wading is unnecessary.

Waimea Stream

Location and access   Rises in the hills south of Lumsden, flows south-east and enters the Mataura River at Mandeville. Can be reached from roads south of Balfour and Riversdale, such as Waimea Valley Road, Nine Mile Road and Crooked Road.

Season   1 October–30 April.

Restrictions   The bag limit is 4 trout.

This stream has been straightened to improve farm drainage, and during summer parts of the stream will often dry. It holds small brown trout but is not highly recommended, though there are a few good holes well upstream in the vicinity of Fairplace Station.

Otamita Stream

Location and access   Rises in the Hokonui Hills, follows an easterly course and joins the Mataura just downstream from the Waimea at Mandeville. Access from behind Mandeville village, from the Otamita–Mandeville road south of Mandeville, then Otamita Valley Road.

Season   1 October–30 April.

Restrictions   The bag limit is 4 trout.

This very pleasant small stream flows over a rock and gravel bed and holds a good stock of brown trout in the 0.75–1 kg range. The water is lightly tea-coloured, but the stream is highly regarded for the purist dry fly angler. Banks are generally open and fish can be spotted and stalked. Catch and release is recommended.

Appendix: Identification of trout, salmon and char

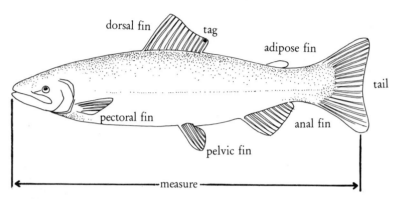

Tagged or marked fish

Brown Trout

(*Salmo trutta*) are the predominate species and widely distributed throughout the South Island. Sea-run fish tend to be silvery in colour, river fish yellowish-green with dark brown and reddish spots, while lake fish have a creamish-yellow body and a speckled appearance. Distinguishing features include:

- Square or slightly forked tail.
- Blue halo around spots especially on gill covers.
- Mouth not black inside.
- Relatively short and deep anal fin.
- Tail not densely spotted.

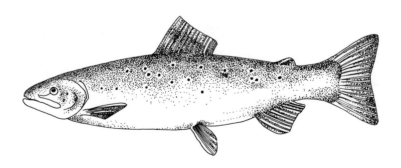

Rainbow Trout

(*Salmo gairdnerii*) inhabit lakes and rivers. There are no sea-run species. Lake-dwelling fish tend to be more silvery in colour. Distinguishing features include:

- Square or slightly forked tail.
- Pinkish-rose tinge on the gill covers and along the lateral line, but no spots on the gill covers.
- Mouth not black inside.
- Short-based anal fin with 8–12 rays.
- Dense black spots on tail, head, back, sides, and dorsal and adipose fins.

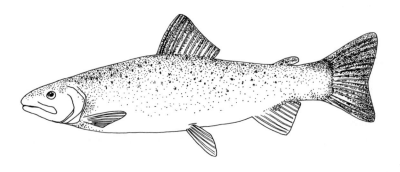

Quinnat, King or Chinook Salmon

(*Oncorhynchus tschawytscha*) were introduced from the West Coast of North America. They are present as landlocked fish in Lake Coleridge and the southern lakes, and as sea-run fish in many South

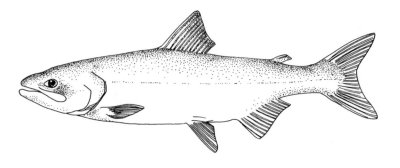

Island rivers where the sea temperature does not rise above 15 degrees C. Lake fish are much smaller. Sea-run fish tend to darken in colour and lose their silvery sheen as they migrate up rivers to spawn. Distinguishing features include:
- Prominently forked tail.
- Mouth black inside between the teeth.
- Long-based low anal fin.
- Oncorhynchus means hooked snout.

Atlantic Salmon
(*Salmo salar*) are present as landlocked fish in Lakes Te Anau, Manapouri, Gunn and Fergus. A spawning run occurs in the Upukerora and Eglinton rivers. These fish are rare, tend to be long and thin, and seldom grow larger than 2 kg. They resemble brown trout but have small, slender, dark spots on the back and sides of the head which are not surrounded by paler haloes, and there are no pale or reddish spots on the sides.

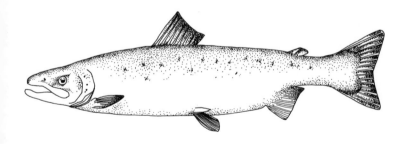

Sockeye Salmon
(*Oncorhynchus nerka*), which were also introduced from the West Coast of North America, are found only in the Waitaki Lakes and Lake Poerua as landlocked resident fish. There is no evidence of a sea-run habit in New Zealand. The mouth is not black between the teeth. Gill rakers are long and numerous (31–43).

Brook Char
(*Salvelinus fontinalis*) are found only in a few small lakes and the headwaters of selected streams. Distinguished by their colourful appearance, they have a dark olive-green vermicular pattern on the back, dorsal fin and upper lobe of the tail, the flank is a silvery purplish pale blue colour while the belly is white tinged with orange. There are also yellow and red spots on the sides. The caudal fin is a little forked and the shortest ray is more than half the length of the longest. There is a pale leading edge to the pelvic and anal fins followed by a strongly contrasting black stripe.

Macinaw
(*Salvelinus namaycush*) are very rare and only found in Lake Pearson. The caudal fin is deeply forked and the shortest ray is less than half the length of the longest. The pale leading edge to the pelvic and anal fin is not followed by a black stripe.